I am grateful to Phil Bates for his assistance in filling in some gaps in my knowledge in relation to the period immediately leading up to the trial and also in relation to the trial itself.

Cover Photo: Coniston Water

A Very Cumbrian Murder
The Tragic Story of the Lady in the Lake

– DOUGLAS RICHARD BINSTEAD –

Printed and bound in England by www.printondemand-worldwide.com

http://www.fast-print.net/bookshop

A VERY CUMBRIA MURDER:
THE TRAGIC STORY OF THE LADY IN THE LAKE
Copyright © Douglas Richard Binstead 2016

All rights reserved

No part of this book may be reproduced in any form by photocopying or any electronic or mechanical means, including information storage or retrieval systems, without permission in writing from both the copyright owner and the publisher of the book.

The right of Douglas Richard Binstead to be identified as the author of this work has been asserted by him in accordance with the Copyright, Designs and Patents Act 1988 and any subsequent amendments thereto.

A catalogue record for this book is available from the British Library

Paperback ISBN 978-178456-351-6
Hardback ISBN 978-178456-352-3

First published 2016 by
FASTPRINT PUBLISHING
Peterborough, England.

A VERY CUMBRIAN MURDER

THE TRAGIC STORY OF THE LADY IN THE LAKE

Introduction

The murder of Carol Ann Park is, by common consent, one of the most infamous cases in English criminal history. It relates to the brutal killing of a young woman, the mother of three small children, by a cold and calculating husband. The husband methodically, painstakingly and elaborately trusses up the body and deposits it in the dark and murky depths of a picturesque English lake, where it lies for 21 years before its fortuitous discovery. There have been many other equally callous murders, and some where similarly great pains have been taken to try to ensure that the crime and the body would remain undetected. There have been few, however, where the crime has remained concealed for so long, and, indeed, where so many years have passed before the perpetrator has been brought to book.

What really sets this case apart, however, is the fact that the murder of Carol Park was not the first such tragedy that had befallen her family in recent times. A little over seven years before Carol's death, her sister Christine, then aged 17 and the mother of a very young child, was murdered by her boyfriend, John Rapson. There have been cases where members of the same family have been murdered by the same person at the same time – one thinks, for example, of the multiple killings by Jeremy Bamber in Essex in 1986, and by William Hughes in the Pottery Cottage murders in Derbyshire in 1977. As far as I am aware, however, for two sisters to be slaughtered by two different men in two totally unrelated murders, seven years apart, is a situation completely without precedent. It is a gross understatement to describe Carol's murder as an "appalling coincidence", as it was so described at the trial of Gordon Park. If this double tragedy was not enough, it is aggravated by the fact that Carol's family was blighted by other tragedies: her brother dying in infancy and a niece dying in her twenties of leukaemia.

I did not arrive in Barrow-in-Furness until 1982, and knew nothing of the affair of the missing Carol Park until that day in the summer of 1997 when her body was retrieved from Coniston Water. From that moment on, however, I became fascinated with the case and with the unique circumstances of the murder and the tragic background. Its uniqueness and the dark and mysterious character of the case, enhanced by the 'Arthurian' sobriquet given to it by the police – the Lady in the Lake- ensured that it would attract the attention of the national media. These factors alone encouraged me, at an early stage, to contemplate writing this book at some later date, but what finally provoked me into undertaking the task was my reading in 2015 of a book by one Dr Sandra Lean.

Dr Lean, an academic, is the author of a book published in 2008 entitled *No Smoke! The Shocking Truth About British Justice*. As the title might suggest, the work is a full-frontal attack on every aspect of our criminal justice system, from the nature of police investigations into serious crime to the working of the jury system. In one chapter, the case of Gordon Park is singled out as a suitable example of a flawed investigation and, ultimately, of a wrongful conviction. Her assault upon what she perceives as an inadequate police inquiry into the murder, the conduct of prosecuting counsel, the lack of any cogent evidence against Park, and the misconceived verdict of the jury, is scathing and relentless.

I read Dr Lean's book and was left with a feeling of total exasperation and incredulity at the enormity of her prejudiced assertions, her glib dismissal of the case against Park and her apparent lack of understanding of how police investigations and the criminal justice system worked. I embarked upon my own book in an attempt to redress the balance and to demonstrate how compelling was the case and how right the jury were to return a guilty verdict. The reader must decide who has right on their side – Dr Lean or the jury!

In 1997 I was the Branch Crown Prosecutor in the Cumbrian Branch of the northern area of the Crown Prosecution Service and, as such, responsible for the portfolio of criminal cases that arose in the county. I was involved in the Park case from the outset, actively engaged in the review of the evidence and the preparation of the case papers, and, as it turned out, the vain attempt to persuade my superiors that the prosecution should proceed. I also had what was, for me, the unwanted task of issuing the formal notice that put an end to the case in early 1998. After that, however, I took a part in the happier process of the reappraisal of the case in 2003, and the decision to resurrect the prosecution against Gordon Park. Although other responsibilities took me away from the subsequent lead-up to the trial in 2004/5, I kept up with the developments in the preparation of the case for trial and the course of the trial itself.

The content of my book is drawn from my intimate knowledge of the evidence that was gathered by the police in the investigation of 1997 and in the later enquiry, either from my very strong recollection of that evidence or from extensive notes that I compiled at the time of reviewing that evidence. I have used that knowledge of the evidence to show, hopefully, how there was, as the Court of Appeal later put it, a "strong circumstantial case" against Park, and how the verdict of the jury was right and proper.

It would be misleading and inappropriate to deal with Carol's disappearance in 1976, and the later investigations and the trial, in a vacuum. Context here is very important. The narrative, therefore, covers Carol's origins, Gordon's background, the years of their courtship and the gradual disintegration of their marriage between 1971 and 1976. One cannot readily appreciate what happened in July 1976 without this information. There then follows what is known as the 'Missing Person' inquiry, and, although it is easy to make judgements with the benefit of hindsight, the reader may wish to consider whether the police response to Carol's disappearance was an apposite and adequate one.

Of necessity, the book must deal with what happened in the 'limbo' between 1976 and 1997. This period is entirely about Gordon Park, his disastrous second marriage and the obvious peace and contentment he finds in his successful third marriage. There are, initially at least, significant further clues to be found as to Gordon's character, and also evidence of his ability to obliterate Carol from his memory and 'airbrush' her out of his life.

The next phase of the story covers the dramatic discovery of Carol's body in August 1997, the charging of Gordon with her murder and the anti-climax of the case against him being dropped for "insufficiency of evidence". The last phase is the emergence of fresh evidence, the re-charging of Park and his trial, conviction and sentence. The final chapter is given over to examining and confronting the extreme views of Dr Sandra Lean, on the criminal justice system in general and the Park case in particular.

★ ★ ★

The murder of Carol Park rightly deserves its reputation as a notorious and unique case. It does, however, share some of its uniqueness with some other cases. The distinctive Cumbrian landscape, with its many fells and lakes, offers an obvious attraction to the would-be 'wife murderer' who thinks he may have the recipe for the 'perfect murder' and the opportunity to dispose of his victim in a manner that will prevent forever detection of his crime and of the body. Carol Park was not the first murder victim to be retrieved from the murky depths of a Lake District body of water, and she will surely not be the last…

In this sense this was indeed 'A Very Cumbrian Murder'.

Chapter One

Carol and Gordon Park: The Early Years

17 July 1976 was almost certainly the last day in the life of Carol Ann Park. No-one can reliably claim to have seen her alive after that date. We know no more of her until her dead body is recovered from Coniston Water 21 years later, on 13 August 1997.

What is certain is that she was born on 18 December 1945, the daughter of a wartime Land Girl and an unknown father. Her mother was one Elsie Saunders, 24 years of age at this time, and who had been born and raised in Bristol. Elsie had married a local man, George Saunders, at the beginning of the War. George seems to have been a serving soldier for most of the War and it appears that he was in Burma at the time that Carol must have been conceived. The identity of the father remained and remains unknown. Elsie was 'sent away' somewhere to have the baby, apparently to conceal the fact of her pregnancy from her husband.

This scenario must have been far from uncommon in 1945/1946 – husband returns from the War, finds in his absence that his wife has borne another man's child, 'wronged' husband rejects the child, the 'father' is no longer on the scene. Carol is therefore 'put up for adoption' in order, no doubt, to save Elsie and George's marriage.

The adoption takes place far from Bristol, in a remote town at the foot of the Furness peninsula. Barrow-in-Furness, now part of Cumbria, was in those days in Lancashire. The adoptive parents are Stanley and Winifred Price, who live in the Roose area of Barrow, and their son Ivor, then six years of age, recalls a meeting at the family home with a young woman and a man wearing an army uniform: he assumes these are the natural parents, but almost certainly the man is George Saunders. The formal adoption of Carol occurred in January or February 1946.

Despite the 'personal touch' involved in the adoption of Carol, and despite an apparent desire on Carol's part later in life to trace her birth mother, it seems she was never destined to meet Elsie, George or indeed her natural father. Elsie and George's marriage did survive for a time but they divorced some ten years later, shortly after emigrating to New Zealand. Elsie died in December 1985 having had one further child by her marriage to George and two more by a second marriage. It seems unlikely that any of these children have been aware that they had a half-sister in the north-west of England. Elsie had two sisters still living in 1997, both of whom were aware of Carol's existence, but neither of whom had ever met her.

The family life of the Prices was tinged with tragedy. This is in fact an understatement. Of the four children of Stanley and Winifred, including Carol, only one lived beyond the age of 30. Their second son Brian died in infancy from a heart condition. As we shall see, their natural daughter Christine met a violent end at the age of 17. Their eldest son Ivor had three daughters, but the eldest, Deborah, also died tragically young from leukaemia, whilst still in her twenties.

Carol, however, appears to have enjoyed a reasonably happy childhood. She was readily accepted into the family, and excelled academically at school. In particular, from an early age she displayed a musical talent and by the age of 12 was regularly playing the organ in St Luke's church in Roose. She passed the eleven-plus examination and attended what was then Barrow Girls Grammar School, achieving good qualifications and also showing an aptitude for learning foreign languages, attaining fluency in French and German. Her progression to higher education, however, was halted at this time by the sudden death of her adoptive father Stanley in 1963, and instead of moving on to university, Carol felt the need to look for full-time employment locally.

Carol found employment as a clerk in the Finance Department at Barrow town hall and remained there until she did finally resume her education by enrolling on a teacher training course at Matlock College in Derbyshire in September 1964.

During her time at the town hall Carol continued to live at home with her adoptive mother and younger sister Christine, but she enjoyed an active and flourishing social life. She is described at this time as being about five feet two inches in height, of proportionate build, as having dark wavy hair and always smartly and fashionably dressed. She is gregarious and popular, and a word that constantly recurs when described by those that knew her is "vivacious". Her brother Ivor refers to her having several boyfriends, but it is in this period that she forms a more permanent relationship with a young man she had first known during her school days – Gordon Park.

★ ★ ★

A Very Cumbrian Murder

Gordon Park, unlike Carol, was a native of Barrow-in-Furness and, indeed, other than his time in prison, was to spend his entire life in the town or its immediate vicinity. He was born on 25 January 1944, the middle child of Sydney and Elsie Park, and had an elder sister, Barbara, and a younger brother, Sydney Terrance. The family lived at various addresses in Barrow until settling in 1960 at a house in Rampside, Barrow, which was conveniently close to Roa Island boat club. Sydney Senior was a member of the club and his enthusiasm for sailing was passed on to his sons, both of whom were involved in this pursuit from an early age.

By the early 1960s the family was enjoying quite a comfortable and prosperous lifestyle. From small beginnings, Sydney Senior had established a painting and decorating business which was operating out of three shops in Barrow, and, for a while at least, from one in the neighbouring town of Ulverston. The business was known as Sydney C. Park Limited and eventually became Sydney C. Park & Sons when Gordon and his brother joined the firm.

The family owned a large static caravan which was sited at Torver, a village close to Coniston Water. Local solicitor, Robert Forrester, a lifelong friend of Park senior, also had a caravan on the same site and Robert's son, also Robert, appears to have been friendly with Gordon (although the latter would have been five years older than Robert Junior). Father Park owned a fourteen-foot sailing dinghy which he would keep on a trailer, either near the caravan or close to the lake, and he and the two boys would sail the boat on Coniston Water. On one occasion, in about 1958, one of these sailing trips attained both local and national publicity when their boat capsized and Park

Senior, Gordon and a family friend, Tony Salton, had to be rescued by Leo Villa, who was the chief mechanic for Donald Campbell. Campbell, of course, lost his own life on the same lake in January 1967 whilst attempting to break his own water speed record in *Bluebird*. Despite the fact that the approximate location of his body must have been known, Campbell's corpse had not been recovered from Coniston Water by the time of Carol Park's disappearance more than nine years later (it was eventually found in 2001). Perhaps the significance of this fact was not lost upon Gordon Park?

Gordon attended local primary schools and ultimately Barrow Grammar School – now part of Furness Academy. It was at the grammar school that Gordon met other boys, who would become and remain friends throughout his life; in particular Ernie Shaw, Paul Shaw (no relation), Malcolm Short, Ian Rawlinson and Barrie Turner. Some of these shared his enthusiasm, to a greater or lesser degree, for sailing, and some shared a later interest in rock-climbing. Gordon was also at one time a keen scout.

Interestingly, from my own experience of scouting, learning about and using various knots was an important part of one's development in the movement, and certainly would have been at the time Gordon Park was a scout. One learnt how to tie the sheet-bend, clove-hitch, reef knot, round-turn-and-two-half-hitches, bowline, sheep-shank, as well as various 'lashings' (for tying two staves or pieces of wood together). My own recollection, also from my rock-climbing days, was that the two most commonly used knots in this activity were the bowline and the figure-of-eight. I have never been a sailor but I have heard that many of these knots are also basic to that pursuit. From an early age, Gordon Park would have become exposed to and been very accustomed to the tying and application of a great number of knots, something that would have set him apart from the great majority of the population as few people would have been involved in more than the first of these activities, let alone all three!

Of his friends from Barrow Grammar School, Paul Shaw, Ian Rawlinson and Malcolm Short all shared Gordon's enthusiasm for sailing. They sailed with him from Roa Island boat club, and Ian also recalls trips in Park Senior's boat on Coniston Water.

Another sailing companion was Rodney Whiteman who met Gordon through Ernie Shaw. Rodney also became one of Gordon's rock-climbing partners at this time, as did Paul Shaw. Rodney also introduced Harry Turner to this group and the four of them used to climb regularly in the Lake District, and there was also a trip to the Pyrenees. Gordon seems to have been the designated driver for the group, using the works van belonging to his father. Rodney Whiteman in particular comments that Gordon was "very proficient" in the tying of the knots used in their sailing and climbing activities.

Gordon's brother Sydney and his close friends, of course, would have been aware of any 'romantic attachments' on his part, and the general consensus was that he did not have a lot of girlfriends in his late teens. Sydney recalls that Gordon's "first" girlfriend was one Jennifer Shaw. By a strange twist of fate, more than 20 years later she would become his third wife.

Fate was to play its first card, however, in or about 1964. Susan Dampier, a friend of Carol's from their schooldays, threw a party at her home in Leece. She also knew Gordon, with whom she had had a brief but unsuccessful 'fling', and he was invited, along with some of his friends. Carol came on her own. Whether or not their eyes met 'across a crowded room', Gordon and Carol came together at this point and, according to Susan, seemed to "get on". It seems however that they were not entirely strangers as it is apparent the two of them had known each other during their schooldays. In any event, their relationship starts here and they continued to see each other after the party. Indeed, before Carol had left Barrow for Matlock College they had become engaged…

★ ★ ★

By October 1964, Gordon Park, by now working in the family business, and Carol Ann Price, training to be a school teacher, were an 'item'. They were two very different people. Opposites may attract, but 'opposites' they certainly were. Without exception, Carol's friends and acquaintances and, indeed, Gordon's friends and siblings, paint the same picture of Carol. She is "vivacious", "good-natured", "very friendly", "outgoing" and the "life and soul of the party". No-one has a negative observation to make about her. By contrast, Gordon is not depicted in such a flattering light. Not surprisingly, perhaps, his own friends do not at least run him down – he is described by them as "quiet", "serious", and "intense". One friend refers to there being "nothing striking" about him; another states that his approach was "always to make a good job of everything he tried to do". Damning him with faint praise perhaps! But significantly, another friend says that he could be "dogmatic" and unyielding once he had formed an opinion about anything in particular. Carol's friends who knew Gordon are generally silent about his character and personality, although one refers to him as being "unpredictable".

Other than this, however, there is no hint at this time in his life of there existing any darker side to his character, and, indeed, his friends claim that he is even-tempered and without any aggressive tendencies.

Carol attended Matlock College in Derbyshire between September 1964 and June 1967, leaving with a teaching qualification. From what we know about her, it is unsurprising that she was popular with fellow students and that she made a lot of friends, although mainly female. Her closest college friend appears to have been Rosemary Farmer. Rosemary soon became aware that Carol had a boyfriend back in Barrow. It is often the case that relationships founder or wither on the vine when couples become separated because one or other of them leaves home to go to college or university, but, in this case, it seems that Gordon and Carol's relationship remained strong throughout the three years of Carol's "absence". Rosemary recalls that Gordon would send Carol a red rose every week, and that Carol would become quite upset if the delivery was late or did not arrive.

Rosemary eventually met Gordon at a college summer ball at the end of either the first or second year of their course. Knowing Carol quite well by this time, she is "surprised" by Gordon's character – to her he seemed "unemotional, deep and intense" and "very domineering" with Carol. Moreover, Carol, she says, at this time was "emotionally insecure", having recently discovered that she had been adopted, and resentful that her adoptive parents had never told her this. Nonetheless, it seems to Rosemary that they are "happy together". She does however sound a discordant note. Carol, she says, at one time confided to her a suspicion that Gordon may have been having an "affair" back in Barrow, although her suspicion is apparently never confirmed. Furthermore, Rosemary becomes aware that Carol herself is involved in a "close relationship" in her final year with a college lecturer called Charles Cook, a relationship that did not, however, survive the end of Carol's course. Shades of things to come and the seeds of future disharmony!

Whatever potential difficulties may be simmering in the background, on the face of it the Park/Price relationship seems to be on solid ground in the summer of 1967. There is a lavish 21st birthday party for Carol at the Park home in December 1966, which Rosemary Farmer attends, and Gordon has thrown himself into building the future matrimonial home.

The construction of *Bluestones* is a 'tour de force'. 'Construction' is the right word since the property was built almost entirely by volunteer labour, with Gordon Park leading from the front. In the mid-1960s there was a national company operating a business of selling World War Two 'prefabs'; Gordon bought two of these and converted them into a three-bedroom bungalow. The property was constructed adjacent to and overlooking the tarn in the village of Leece, outside Barrow. Several of Gordon's friends and one or two others assisted in the building work – including Ernie Shaw, Rodney Whiteman, and Paul Shaw. Harry Turner, an electrician, carried out the wiring of the property. Rosemary Farmer, who visited the bungalow in the summer of 1967, is clearly impressed by the soundness of its construction, which she describes as "meticulous and very careful". Knowing Gordon's character, as we do by now, we would expect nothing less! By July 1967, *Bluestones* is almost complete and is habitable.

Carol's brother, Ivor Price, recalls that Carol had told him, when she was no more than 16 years old, that she would never have to struggle in life as she "would marry into money". In 1967, he says, the Park business was still flourishing. The Parks were a prosperous family. Gordon was "a man of property". Carol was about to make a 'good marriage'.

On 28 July 1967, Gordon Park and Carol Ann Price were married in Barrow at Rampside Parish Church…

Chapter Two

1967 to 1974: Portrait of a Failing Marriage

Although it would be wrong to suggest that the union of Gordon and Carol was doomed from the outset, there were already in 1967 the signs of potential future discord, in particular her tendencies to promiscuity. Over the next few years, however, there were to be a number of developments which would put the relationship under severe stress, and ultimately rend it asunder.

Initially, however, the marriage appeared for all the world to be a happy and harmonious one. The pair were comfortably off with Gordon continuing to work in the family business and Carol soon finding employment after qualifying as a teacher in the summer of 1967. Certainly by September 1967 she was working at Victoria County Junior School in Barrow.

Rosemary Farmer, Carol's friend from college, visited *Bluestones* a number of times in this period and thought the pair appeared to "be getting on well".

Mary Robinson and her husband David lived in Leece from April 1967, and because of the proximity of their house with *Bluestones* they struck up a close friendship with the Parks. They socialised often, regularly exchanging visits to each other's homes. Mrs Robinson found Gordon to be occasionally "moody" and uncommunicative, but generally pleasant, and Carol vivacious and friendly.

Desmond McWilliams, who had been at school and in the scouts with Gordon, also moved to Leece with his new wife about Easter 1967 and renewed his acquaintanceship with Gordon. The McWilliams attended several parties at *Bluestones* in these early years, although they were not as close to the Parks as the Robinsons. Desmond describes Gordon as "careful and serious" and Carol as "bubbly and outgoing", but saw them as seeming to "work well together" and appearing to be "very happy".

Another aspect of the Parks' social activity at this time was their membership of the Barrow Round Table (or of the partner organisation, the Ladies' Circle, in Carol's case). The Round Table is a social networking and charitable body open to all men aged between 18 and 45 (41 in those days). Members enjoy social and community service activities and also become involved in fundraising for charities, and members' wives automatically qualify for the sister body, the Ladies' Circle. Members tend to be drawn mainly from local business and professions, and Gordon Park would probably have known many of his fellow Round Tablers before joining. He appears to have joined in 1964 and, after their marriage, he and Carol clearly attended many of the club's social occasions. According to Philip Fanshawe, who joined at the same time as Gordon, the Parks ceased being members at some point between 1970 and 1975. They appeared to still be members in 1970, the year that Hazel Fanshawe became president of the Ladies' Circle. She became aware that the clubs changed character at about this time, with a culture of 'wife-swapping' starting to develop. One may have thought that this might have appealed to the gregarious and free-spirited Carol, but Hazel did not think that the Parks were taking part in such activities!

As well as a busy social life, Gordon continued to indulge his passion for sailing, although he maintained later when being interviewed by the police that he did not go very often to Coniston at this time and was mainly 'crewing' for others at Roa Island sailing club. His neighbours, however, were aware that he was building a sailing dinghy on his driveway at *Bluestones*. It seems that he had given up rock-climbing by the time he was married, in common with many others attracted to the sport in their youth but abandoning it when assuming the responsibilities of marriage and, particularly, of parenthood!

This uneventful existence and lifestyle of relative marital harmony was then turned upside down in April 1969 by an appalling tragedy, an occurrence that was to trigger or foreshadow a series of other events that were to ultimately undermine the relationship of Gordon and Carol and then to lead on to the ultimate tragedy of their story.

★ ★ ★

At the age of 16, Carol's sister Christine became pregnant, but never revealed to her family the identity of the father of the child Vanessa, who was born on 6 March 1968. Christine continued to live with her mother on Roose Road, Barrow. The father was possibly John Paul Rapson, aged 17 at the time of Vanessa's birth, and indeed he later maintained that Christine had told him that he was the father. Rapson had been involved in an 'on-off' relationship with Christine for some time, although he claimed that she did have other boyfriends as well over this period.

A Very Cumbrian Murder

When Vanessa was only 13 months old, in April 1969, Christine was brutally murdered in her home by the same John Rapson. Christine's mother was in the house at the time and managed to escape and alert a neighbour who in turn contacted the police. Rapson was later convicted of murder and sentenced to life imprisonment, although he was released in September 1976 having served only seven years of the prison term.

The Price family was to lose two of its members to violent and premature deaths. But this is to grossly understate the position. The tragedy of the Prices was one of monumental and unprecedented significance. There are a number of well-documented instances of several family members being slaughtered by one man in one bloody murderous enterprise. The cases of Jeremy Bamber, who murdered five of his family in 1985 and the Pottery Cottage murders in Derbyshire in 1976, spring to mind. But for two sisters to be killed, seven years apart, by two different men, who had no connection with each other and had almost certainly never met, is, as far as I am aware, an occurrence that is entirely unique in the annals of criminal conduct.

The immediate result of Christine's demise, of course, was that little Vanessa was left parentless. Initially she continued to live with her grandmother in the house on Roose Road, but Mrs Price was not in good health, and Ivor Price and his wife Maureen felt that they could not realistically take Vanessa in as Maureen had just given birth to their third daughter. Vanessa was therefore taken into the care of the local authority and went to reside in a children's home, Dunlop House, on Abbey Road, Barrow.

It is now that events take a further significant twist. A few months after Christine's death, Gordon and Carol commenced proceedings to adopt Vanessa and before the end of the year the adoption was formalised and Vanessa went to live at *Bluestones*. The rest of the Price family was most unhappy with what they regarded as the furtive manner in which the proceedings were launched and pursued. Neither Ivor nor his mother were consulted about the Parks' intentions, and by the time Ivor discovered what was happening and sought legal advice about the enterprise, it was too late and the adoption had happened.

Notwithstanding the secrecy with which Gordon and Carol conducted themselves, it seems that adopting Vanessa was an appropriate and compassionate act on their part. No-one else in the family seemed to be able or willing to take her in, and the alternative would have been to leave her in the care of the local authority, no doubt ultimately to be fostered or adopted by strangers. Certainly Vanessa's situation would have struck a chord with Carol, bearing in mind her own childhood history.

Despite the ill-feeling that the adoption proceedings engendered with Ivor and his mother, the former seems to have regarded himself as always being close to Carol. Interestingly enough, however, Carol confided in a colleague at Victoria Road School at this time, that she "had no time at all for her family", that she was never allowed to forget that she was adopted and that she "was always supposed to be grateful". Perhaps this might explain the Parks' reluctance to consult with the Prices about adopting Vanessa, and it may well be, of course, that Carol saw an opportunity to bestow upon this small girl the love and kindness that she regarded herself as having been denied in a similar situation.

In interviews with the police in 1997, Gordon made it clear that the decision to adopt Vanessa was a joint one, and that at the time it seemed to be "right and proper". He expressed no regrets about the decision, but it triggered a series of events which, in hindsight he felt, were mistakes and started to lead to the breakdown of the marital relationship.

★ ★ ★

At the time that Vanessa was formally adopted, Carol must have already been pregnant with the Parks' first natural child, as Jeremy Park was born on 30 March 1970. But, according to what Gordon said later to the police, the decision to start their own family was made whilst they were still engaged in the adoption proceedings. They had not intended to have children this early in the marriage, but then decided to bring the whole process forward once they had made their plans regarding Vanessa, so that the children would be close in age and the family would be complete. After Jeremy's birth, Rachel Park followed soon after, being born on 27 May 1971.

Acquiring three young children in less than 18 months, Gordon regarded, with the benefit of hindsight, as a "mistake". "We were too young. We were not ready" he later told the police; "we hadn't known each other long enough". He felt the experience "took a great deal out of Carol" and "she would become dissatisfied with me". This he felt was where things "started to go wrong".

A stressful period at home for the Parks was also to coincide with strains for Gordon in the workplace and in his relationship with his parents. The latters' marriage was breaking down at this time and their increasingly acrimonious relationship was having an adverse impact on the family business. Although it was still a profitable concern, and Gordon stood to inherit the enterprise in due course with his brother, he found the situation intolerable, and whilst Carol was at home giving birth, or preparing to give birth, to one or other of the two younger children, he left Sydney C. Park and Sons and took up employment with other firms in Barrow – firstly Listers, and then Ferrantis. It seems these jobs did not last much more than 12 months, for in autumn 1972 Gordon enrolled as a student at Charlotte Mason College in Ambleside, having decided that he wanted to train and qualify as a teacher. In the same year, and possibly at the same time, Carol returned to teaching, after the birth of her children, at Broughton-in-Furness Church of England School.

During the two- or three-year period following the birth of Rachel Park, there began to appear outward signs that indicated, or might have indicated, that all was not well in the marriage.

Carol Hewitt worked with Gordon Park at Ferrantis; he was her supervisor. She portrays him as sullen, uncommunicative and often pre-occupied – "he would walk around the factory floor looking as though he had something on his mind all the time". He also had a "condescending attitude". She also recalls one occasion when he completely lost his temper, shouting and "going mad" in front of other employees.

Ivor Price describes Gordon at this time as "controlling", requiring Carol, who was by 1973 the family 'bread-winner', to hand over her wages to Gordon; despite the family's comparatively financially straitened circumstances, Gordon was spending money to indulge his passion for sailing. Maureen Price perceived that there was friction between Gordon and Carol over "money matters", but that Gordon would continue to spend a good deal of money pursuing his hobby.

Hazel Butters, who later became the second wife of Sidney Park Senior, was by mid-1972 living with Sidney, whose wife had left him in 1971. She appears to have formed an unfavourable impression of Gordon from the very first. She portrays him as ostentatious and materialistic, despite the family's lack of money, and "selfishly" spending on equipment for his boats and on a new car for himself. She recalls Vanessa and the younger children complaining that, on a family holiday in France, they had run out of money and were reduced to eating bread and jam for the last few days! At the same time, she found Carol to be friendly, and supportive of her when she joined the family.

Carol's college friend, Rosemary Farmer, had continued to maintain contact with Carol. It began to become evident to her, through telephone conversations with, and letters from, Carol at this time, that the Parks' relationship was becoming strained. It was clear to her that whilst Gordon was in full-time education they were struggling to make ends meet. At one point in 1973, Carol confided in her that she suspected Gordon "was having an affair". She had no more than suspicion, however, and indeed there is no evidence that this was the case. After this revelation, which came at a time when Carol and the children were visiting her, Rosemary only went back to *Bluestones* on one other occasion, in 1974, where she found that the atmosphere in the house was "tense" and there was "constant bickering" between Carol and Gordon. She never went to Leece again.

Jill Heaps, a school friend of Carol's, and someone she had known as "even-tempered and bouncy", chanced to meet Carol in Dalton Road in Barrow, shortly after Rachel had been born. She is surprised by what she describes as a "noticeable difference" in Carol's attitude. She did not appear to be happy and all her "bounce" had gone. Jill recalls a remark from Carol that she had "had enough lads" and forms the impression that she was not just referring to her son!

Following Jeremy's birth in 1970, Sharon Pickavance, a girl of 15 or 16 years of age who lived in Leece, would occasionally babysit for the Parks. She found Carol, as many others did, to be pleasant and friendly. She seems to have no time for Gordon, however, who she describes as a "bighead" and who seemed to her to be jealous of Carol, who he would openly refer to as a "know-it-all school teacher". It is possible that her opinion of Gordon might have been coloured by an incident that occurred on one occasion when the Parks had returned from a night out. Whilst Carol was out of the room, Sharon claims that Gordon made an improper suggestion to her. After that Sharon did not babysit again and never went to the house whilst Gordon might have been present.

As far as Gordon himself was concerned, when interviewed in 1997 and 2004 by the police he did not acknowledge any specific responsibility on his part for the deterioration of the relationship. He denied that he was materialistic or extravagant. His hobby cost him next to nothing, he said, because he was only "crewing" for others. There were no expensive holidays, they avoided hire purchase agreements, cars were paid for in cash. The decisions to have children and for him to start a teacher training course were taken jointly. He felt their sex life was perfectly normal and that he was not, in any way, inadequate – but, he mused, he must have been "inadequate" as otherwise Carol would not have "gone elsewhere".

By mid-1973, however, it is evident that Carol had indeed "gone elsewhere"...

★ ★ ★

Back teaching at Broughton-in-Furness Church of England School in the autumn of 1972, Carol had a lift to her place of work each day with John Wilkes, now the head teacher at a school in the same village, Broughton Tower. Carol knew John from a brief period when she had been a supply teacher at a school in Barrow a little earlier and he and his wife were friendly with both the Parks. John was also a student at the Open University and it was probably in late 1972 that Carol made the fateful decision to enrol with the same body, ostensibly to improve her teaching qualifications and her career prospects. One Colin Foster was already a student with the OU; in 1973 a man called David Brearley also enrolled.

John Wilkes says there was nothing inappropriate about his relationship with Carol. They talked a lot on the car journeys but never about personal matters. John, however, recalls Carol coming to a meeting of Open University students at Broughton Tower School in 1973, accompanied by another man "who was not her husband", a scenario he found quite embarrassing. The "other man" was almost certainly Colin Foster. Presumably John formed the view that the pair were more than just colleagues, hence his embarrassment!

Gordon Park had another view about Carol's association with John Wilkes. He believed that Carol and Wilkes had some kind of "emotional entanglement" and he confronted the latter with his suspicions. Mr Wilkes says that Gordon initially came to see him at his home at a time when Carol would have been away at weekend school as part of her Open University course. John claims that Park appeared to be "surprised to see him", the implication being that Gordon expected Carol and Wilkes to be away together! Wilkes was sufficiently concerned by the visit to go to *Bluestones* in turn in an attempt to "clear the air". He felt satisfied that he had managed to persuade Park that there was nothing untoward in his association with Carol.

Park later told the police that he believed Wilkes when he asserted that there had been no "physical contact" between Carol and himself. Indeed, he maintained that John Wilkes was "dead straight" and "an upright, decent, honourable man". It seems entirely unlikely that John Wilkes and Carol had any sexual involvement. There is no evidence that he was any more perhaps than a confidante for Carol, or, as Park himself suggested, some kind of "father-figure" (he was about 15 years older than Carol). In any event, for much of this period Carol's real interest lay elsewhere…

★ ★ ★

Colin Sidney Foster was about ten years older than Carol. He had been in the navy but by 1972 he was employed in the shipyard in Barrow. He lived at that time in Askam-in-Furness with his wife of 15 years, Isabella, and their children. In 1971 he commenced a course with the Open University, continuing to work full-time but completing coursework in the evenings and at weekends.

Local OU students were in the habit of organising regular social events for their number, and Colin attended many of these, sometimes, but not always, in company with his wife. It was at one such event that he met John Wilkes, and at another, Carol Park.

Before long, Colin found himself attracted to the lively and outgoing Carol, and at some point, probably in late 1972, they embarked upon an extra-marital affair which was to last for some 18 months. Whilst in the early days they would meet probably once a month, as time went on their trysts would become much more frequent, and often more than once a week. Colin had met Gordon Park at the social events, and found him to be an entirely different character from his wife – a complete "opposite" in fact. He became convinced that Carol and Gordon were entirely unsuited for each other and that "things weren't right at home" between them.

It seems that the Parks and Colin and Isabella went out together as a 'foursome' on at least a couple of occasions, and, if one takes at face value what Gordon later told the police in interviews, their relationship to each other was not entirely conventional. Gordon describes one occasion, either at *Bluestones* or at the Fosters' home, where a situation arose where Carol and Colin "were in one bedroom" and Gordon and Isabella were together in another. Echoes of the wife-swapping culture at the Round Table perhaps! Gordon claims that nothing of a sexual nature occurred between Mrs Foster and himself, and he believes that the same applied as far as the other two were concerned. From the content of this part of the interview, however, it seems quite plain that Gordon at this time already knew or at least strongly suspected that Colin and Carol were having an affair, as he indicates that after this occasion he told Carol that what was happening "wasn't right" and that she agreed that she "wouldn't see him anymore". Even if the Parks hadn't arrived at the situation of an 'open marriage' at this point, it is nonetheless strange behaviour, and it makes Gordon's conduct in relation to the Fosters at a later date appear perhaps less bizarre than it does at first sight.

Neither Colin nor his wife allude to this odd episode, although Colin at least refers to the four of them going out for a meal and then returning in separate cars, but with Carol and Colin in one vehicle, and Gordon and Isabella in the other. He cannot explain why this occurred.

Whether or not Gordon had previously known about the affair, or whether he believed it had ended, there came a point, probably in early 1974, that he decided that there was an affair or that the affair was still ongoing, as the case may be. He contacted Colin's wife and outlined his suspicions. Isabella claims that she didn't believe Gordon at first but was then persuaded of the truth of the matter when Gordon told her he had had Carol followed by a private detective (almost certainly untrue, as Gordon makes no reference to this when interviewed by the police).

There then ensues a very bizarre sequence of events. Isabella confronts Colin and Colin admits the affair but says it is coming to an end, in any event. Either the same night or shortly afterwards, Carol turns up at the Fosters' home, and she and Colin go off and spend a night at the Swan Hotel at Newby Bridge (on the A590 between Barrow and the M6 motorway). The next day Colin goes home and tells his wife the affair has ended. According to Gordon, Carol returns home at the same time, "rather crestfallen", and the affair is forgiven. Isabella appears to

A Very Cumbrian Murder

be equally forgiving of Colin and their marriage also continues.

That is not, however, the end of the matter. About two months later, Colin says he is contacted by Gordon and is asked to come out and meet him and Carol at a public house in Dalton-in-Furness. Isabella is made aware of the invitation and apparently consents to her husband going to this curious rendezvous. The three meet up as arranged, but Colin and Carol then detach themselves from Gordon and go and sit in Colin's car in the pub carpark. Carol tells Colin that she wants to resume their affair. In the meantime, Gordon drives to Askam and informs Isabella that he has left her husband and Carol together in Dalton. A furious Mrs Foster then persuades a neighbour to drive her to the pub in question. There she confronts Carol, having prevailed on her to alight from Colin's car, and there is an exchange of 'pleasantries' between the two women and some "pushing and shoving". All the while Gordon is sat in his own car, witnessing the spectacle, making no attempt to assist or intervene, but displaying a facial expression which Isabella says "could almost have been a smile". Isabella then gets into Colin's car, but Carol makes no attempt to approach Gordon, instead climbing over a fence into a neighbouring field.

This is still not quite the end of the matter. Although Colin and Isabella are back together as husband and wife, Colin still cannot resist meeting up with Carol a few months later at Keele University where she is on a weekend course and spending the night with her. Isabella only learns of this meeting some months later. It is at this time that Colin decides he needs to leave the Furness area and he and his family move in 1975 to Scotland. He never sees or hears from Carol again.

If the conduct of Carol and Colin is obviously reprehensible, that of Gordon and Isabella is, or appears, strange and enigmatic. In the case of Carol, even if this was her first extra-marital affair (and we certainly cannot be sure about that) she is showing herself to be a young woman who has no scruples about cheating on her husband and, indeed, her previous and subsequent behaviour tend to confirm that she is almost addicted to such conduct. Colin too seems to have entered into the affair willingly and wholeheartedly and, even after he is 'discovered', appears, initially at least, reluctant to abandon the relationship. If we believe what Gordon says, Isabella seems to have connived at inappropriate behaviour by her husband with Carol, and then surprisingly raises no objection to her adulterous husband going off to meet with his erstwhile paramour and her husband in a pub carpark.

It is Gordon's behaviour, however, which is truly bizarre. Or is it? By his own admission he participates in a 'wife-swapping' scenario, even if that proves to be abortive. He seems at this point to already know of his wife's affair but, by his own behaviour, seems to be condoning it. He then sets up a meeting of Carol and Colin (even though the affair is supposed to have been over for a couple of months) contrives to bring Isabella to the scene and then appears to be deriving some voyeuristic pleasure from observing the fall-out from the meeting which he has himself arranged!

Is this not, in fact, the dark side of Gordon starting to emerge? A manipulative 'control freak', a man only too ready to humiliate his wife and exploit her weaknesses, and derive a perverse pleasure from doing so? Ominous and portentous behaviour.

By the same token, Carol's conduct is just as much an omen. Destined to be a serial adulteress, it is really no great surprise that before she has finished her dalliance with Colin Foster she has already embarked upon another yet more serious affair that will strain her marriage to Gordon almost to breaking-point, and will hasten the tragic denouement of their fractured relationship…

Chapter Three

1974 to 1975: The Teesside Interlude

By the mid-point of 1974, whatever tensions simmered below the surface, whatever had gone before, the marriage of Gordon and Carol appeared to most people who knew them as still being founded on a happy and settled relationship. They and their three young children seemed, for all the world, to represent a normal and contented family.

Of the three children, only Vanessa would have been of an age to have had any real memories of home life at this time. She recalls attending Broughton school where Carol worked, travelling there each day in her mother's car. It seems that Gordon had completed his teacher training at about this time and was teaching at South Newbarns Junior School in Barrow. Like Carol, he appears to have had no difficulty in obtaining employment locally.

Whilst Vanessa remembers loud arguments between her parents, these were normally after all the children were in bed, and she doesn't suggest that these detracted from what she describes as and clearly feels was a normal and happy family situation. She recalls being punished on occasions by both her parents for misbehaviour and sometimes this would be physical in the form of smacking. She also refers to being smacked with a "stick" by her father, although this was only as a "last resort". She did not, however, regard her parents as "strict".

Kay Gardner, who was the middle daughter of Ivor Price, and who would be five or six years older than Vanessa, would often go to *Bluestones* with her younger sister to play with the Park children. She describes Gordon as "very strict", making the children eat all their vegetables at mealtimes and smacking his children over the head with the hand when they misbehaved. She puts this down, however, to his being a schoolmaster, and she asserts that she was not frightened of him. She also states that Vanessa, Jeremy and Rachel always appeared to be happy when she saw them.

The Parks' close friends and neighbours, the McWilliams, saw nothing untoward in Gordon and Carol's relationship at this time. According to Desmond, in 1974 they appeared to be getting on well after the birth of the children and the adoption of Vanessa, and he describes their marriage as a "joint effort". He refers to Gordon using the boat he had built for "family days out", and, from talking to the family, he recalls that one of their favourite locations for sailing was Coniston.

Despite outward appearances, it seems likely that the Parks' marriage was on shaky ground by this time, and subsequent events would tend to confirm this. There is, however, no doubt about one matter – both Gordon and Carol were completely devoted to their children. This is borne out by the views and impressions of almost all persons they know or with whom they come into contact. One striking example of this is the observation made by Carol's college friend, Rosemary Farmer. On her last visit to *Bluestones* in early 1974 she witnesses "constant bickering" between Gordon and Carol, although no violent conduct. Unlike others, she was already aware of the strains in the relationship, as Carol had shared her difficulties and problems with her in their regular correspondence. Nonetheless, she makes the point strongly that it is clear that both parents "cared greatly for the children".

It may well be, then, that by the summer of 1974 what was keeping Gordon and Carol together was their mutual love for and devotion to the children. This was the glue that was binding them, but not for much longer...

★ ★ ★

David Brearley was also a school teacher, employed in 1974 by the Sunderland Education Authority, and living in Cleveland. Between 1969 and 1971 he had been a police officer in the Durham Constabulary, but then returned to the teaching career he had left before joining the police service. He had married Margaret Jackson in 1967, but the couple separated in 1973, David retaining the custody of their six-year-old son Michael. Like Carol Park, he also embarked on an Open University course at this time, and, like Carol, as part of the course he attended a summer school in August 1974 at Keele University.

The Open University summer school was tailor-made for the outgoing and independent Carol. However much she was attached to her children, it offered an opportunity to free herself, at least for a while, of the shackles of her domestic existence and give free rein to her undoubted inclination to socialise with others and in particular with the opposite sex. She and Brearley were on the same course at the summer school. They soon met and, according to the latter, "were immediately attracted to each other". Friendship developed into "relationship", although not a sexual relationship at this stage. Brearley maintains that he held back as he was experiencing some guilt because Carol was married. One imagines that the guilt was only on his part.

According to Brearley, Carol was remarkably frank about her sexual history, telling him that she had had several affairs and how her husband was in the habit of "timing" their lovemaking, that he would then give her a critical appraisal of her "performance", something perhaps that has a distinct ring of truth.

It seems clear that either during or shortly after the end of the summer school at Keele, Carol had decided to leave Gordon and embark on a full-blooded affair with David Brearley. She made little or no attempt to keep her intentions, or the affair itself, a secret. On returning to Broughton School after the summer holidays in 1974, Carol told her colleague Maureen Fleming that she had met a man called "Dave" at the Open University course and was going to "live with him" in the north-east. Ivor Price became aware of the affair and at some point in 1974 Carol actually brought Brearley to his home to meet him and their mother. Ivor formed an instant favourable impression of the ex-police officer and felt that he and Carol were "very happy" together.

Carol's departure from *Bluestones* can be dated from 31 August 1974. On this day she became a guest at the High Duddon guest house at Duddon Bridge near Broughton-in-Furness. The guest house was in a fairly remote location in the Duddon valley, and the proprietors at that time were Anne and Derrick Walker. They knew Carol, as their daughter Camilla had been attending Broughton School for some four years, and they also knew Jeremy and Vanessa Park, who were also then pupils at the school. Carol had asked if Derrick could give her a lift to school with the Walker children when the next term started, and

Anne Walker assumed she was taking up residence in the guest house because she had "transport problems". Anne soon became aware, however, that this was not the real reason.

When interviewed by the police in 1997, Gordon initially claimed that he did not know of Carol's whereabouts at first, and that he only knew she had left home when he received a phone call from her whilst he was at work. Desmond McWilliams suggests that Gordon appeared to be "mystified" about where Carol was at this time.

The evidence, however, would tend to indicate quite strongly that Gordon knew exactly where Carol was from 31 August 1974. Both Walkers recall Carol arriving for the first time at High Duddon in a car, driven by a man and with three children as passengers. Whilst neither knew Gordon by sight, Anne Walker, at least, knew and recognised Vanessa and Jeremy as two of the passengers. Gordon would later deny that he had driven Carol to the guest house, but it seems very clear that he was the driver on this occasion, and later in interview he would grudgingly acknowledge that this might have been the case, although it was "unlikely". It would of course have been entirely within character for Gordon to have taken Carol to the guest house – conniving at, facilitating and 'controlling' her departure. Anne Walker even remembers him helping to remove Carol's luggage and her hairdryer from the boot of the car. Scarcely a picture of the devastated, abandoned husband.

Within a day or two of being at High Duddon, Carol unburdened herself to Anne Walker and disclosed that she had left Gordon and the children and was involved in a relationship with David Brearley. Gordon would later

A Very Cumbrian Murder

maintain that it was much later that Carol made any sort of move to obtain custody of the children, but Anne Walker states that Carol told her at this time that she was already "fighting for custody". Given the evidence of Carol's undoubted attachment and devotion to her children, it would seem highly unlikely that she would leave home without embarking on serious attempts to obtain custody.

Gordon later claimed that he had gone to High Duddon to see Carol and had asked her to come home. Anne Walker, however, asserts that no such meeting ever took place. Both Walkers do say, however, that Carol went down to Broughton a number of times to meet Gordon in the Kings Head public house. Anne recalls that the meetings were ostensibly about arrangements for custody of the children, arrangements to which Gordon would not agree. Carol always asked Derrick to come and pick her up after these meetings as she told him that she was too "frightened" to allow Gordon to bring her back, although she never actually made any accusations of violence on his part. Again, at first, Gordon denied that these meetings in Broughton took place, although he later conceded that they "might have done".

Between September and Christmas 1974, the Carol/David relationship was rapidly developing. Within a week of returning to the north-east from summer school, Brearley received a letter from Carol, informing him that she had left Gordon and telling him of her whereabouts. Over the next three months, David travelled over to Broughton a number of times, and on occasions stopped at High Duddon guest house. The pair discussed being together and the practicalities of Carol moving to Teesside. If David had any lingering guilt about their affair, it dissipated when they spent a night together in Kendal and had sex for the first time.

Just before Christmas 1974, after the end of the school term, Carol moved to Teesside and she and Brearley moved into 21 Scott Road, Normanby-on-Tees, together with Brearley's young son. Within a few weeks, Carol had been interviewed for and obtained a teaching post at Sunningdale Special School in Middlesbrough. Brearley describes their relationship at this stage as "absolutely marvellous" and that they were "very much in love".

There was however one cloud hanging over them and, indeed, one that was ultimately to disrupt their domestic bliss. Carol was set upon obtaining custody of her children and, to this end, had embarked upon legal proceedings in Teesside Magistrates' Court…

★ ★ ★

It is not clear how often Carol saw her children whilst she was living at High Duddon, but, according to David Brearley, once she had moved to Teesside, her contact with them was limited. Brearley says that Gordon controlled the times and duration of her access to them and laid down ground rules as to what she could and could not do on her visits. She was not, for example, allowed to take the children to the swimming baths. Also at first, at least, contact could only take place at Carol's mother's house, although Brearley does recall that in 1975 the children were allowed to come to Normanby for a week on one occasion. The restricted access, he says, made Carol very depressed and she would often weep uncontrollably. The children themselves have little or no memory of this period in their lives.

It was in late 1974 or early 1975 that Anne Hollows came briefly in to the lives of the Parks, their children and others connected with the family, including David Brearley. Dr Anne Hollows, as she is now, is a principal lecturer in social work at Sheffield Hallam University, and a figure of both national and international standing in the field of child protection issues. In later 1974, however, she was a young, newly-qualified probation officer employed by Cleveland Probation Service. One of her first tasks was to prepare full reports for the court on the Parks and the children in connection with an application for custody being made by Carol. Her reports would assist the court to make an informed decision regarding the best interests and welfare of the children, and consequently which parent would be best suited to have custody of them. In order to complete the reports, she needed to visit both Carol and Gordon in their respective domestic situations, and interview them, Brearley, the children and members of the immediate Park and Price families.

From speaking to her on the telephone and then interviewing her at Normanby, Anne Hollows' initial impression of Carol was not a favourable one. She felt that she was "not a person of great warmth". However, during the course of the visit, the probation officer's views changed quite dramatically, and she formed the opinion that in fact Carol was entirely the opposite. Dr Hollows realised that what she had originally interpreted as "coldness" was a sign of Carol's anxiety and a desperate need for the children. Mr Brearley she found to be a "very nice man" – calm and capable and warmly affectionate towards Carol. There was nothing about him that caused her concern.

Dr Hollows visited Leece in February 1975 where she met Gordon, the children, Gordon's parents and his brother Terry and his wife, and also Carol's mother, brother Ivor and Maureen Price. She found Gordon to be very "controlling", both in the way that he had organised the day "as if with a schedule" to see that she met all persons who could provide a "supportive account of his parenting ability", and in the way that he had organised the domestic life of his family. She recalls labels on drawers detailing their contents and a timetable on the wall setting out children's bathtimes and a rota for domestic chores. To her he appeared to be "somewhat of a cold character" and to have gone out of his way to impress her on the visit, to portray a lifestyle of affluence. He demonstrated a lot of hostility towards Carol and it was also clear to his visitor that he had been obstructive with regard to allowing Carol access to the children.

To the reader, this presents a familiar portrait of Gordon Park, one that others had formed in the past. At the same time, however, Dr Hollows saw that he was "a very concerned parent" who had done everything that he could that appeared to him to be the best for the children.

The three children Dr Hollows found to be "normal kids", albeit Jeremy was a "little withdrawn". It was Jeremy indeed that left her with probably the most heart-wrenching moment of the visit to Leece. As she was about to depart from *Bluestones,* Jeremy was in bed and she went to say "goodnight" to him. As she did so she says that the boy put his arms round her and said "Can't you stay and be our mummy?".

Anne Hollows makes it quite clear that she found Carol Park a much more personable character than her estranged husband. Gordon himself later observed in his

1997 police interview that it was very plain to him that the probation officer didn't like him. He conceded, however, that the eventual report was favourable to him in the way he cared for and looked after the children. The crux of the matter was of course that, whatever her likes and dislikes, Dr Hollows had to have the welfare of the children as her paramount consideration in advising in her report as to which parent should have custody, and she felt that the trauma of moving them to a different home, one to which they were unaccustomed, outweighed other factors which might favour Carol as the potential custodian. And so it was that on 10 March 1975, at a hearing at Teesside Magistrates' Court, custody of the three children was awarded to Gordon Park.

Gordon himself later concedes that the court's decision was clearly devastating for Carol and that she was visibly very upset in court. Brearley, perhaps in a moment of understatement, says that she subsequently became "very depressed". There seems little doubt that, whether Brearley knew it or not at this point, the court's decision was to doom his relationship with Carol. It is also perhaps no exaggeration to say that, had the decision gone the other way and Carol had secured custody of the children, she would most probably have still been alive today.

There is indeed reason to believe that prior to the court date in March 1975, the relationship between Carol and David Brearley was a stable and happy one. She had adopted his surname and they had a joint bank account. They appeared, for all the world, to be living as 'husband and wife'.

At the time of the court hearing, Gordon himself was in a "relationship" with a divorcee of about his own age. Apart from the inconsequential dalliance with the wife of

Colin Foster, Gordon always denied that he had conducted any "affair" whilst he and Carol were together. Once Carol had departed, however (and it is far from clear whether this was before or after she had gone to Teesside) Gordon instigated an affair of his own.

Judith Walmsley was a native of Barrow, and had been at the girls' grammar school. She knew both Gordon and Carol by sight but was not friendly with them. She moved to Manchester following her marriage but when this failed she returned to Barrow with her young daughter. By coincidence she became friendly with Gordon's brother Terry and his wife and, by way of further coincidence, Carol Park's mother moved into the house next door to her. It was no doubt because of the existence of her friendship with Terry and his wife that Judith became involved with Gordon, but when Gordon asked her to go out with him as part of a foursome with his brother and sister-in-law she scarcely knew him. Gordon, she said, called at her house, completely "out of the blue", and asked her if she wanted to go out with him. Perhaps another example of Gordon's 'controlling' tendencies. Probably he never anticipated rejection?!

The assignation proved successful and within a short time Gordon and Judith were an 'item'. Gordon told Anne Hallows, who met Judith, that their relationship was not a "sexual" one. Judith is silent on the point although she describes it, probably euphemistically, as a "full relationship" and she states that she often stayed at *Bluestones* over the weekends. They were together for several months and it perhaps seems unlikely that two 'thirty-somethings' would never go beyond a mere platonic relationship during this time. Whatever the truth of the matter, however, it may well have suited Gordon's

A Very Cumbrian Murder

purpose in his dealings with Anne Hollows, to have presented his relationship with Judith in this 'Clintonesque' way in an attempt to gain the moral highground over his promiscuous wife?!

According to David Brearley, within a week or two of the court hearing, Carol had become so distraught that she told him she was going to return to Leece "to be with her children". He was "shattered" by her decision but did not try to dissuade her, and Carol packed her bags and left for Cumbria and her family.

★ ★ ★

Judith Walmsley was at *Bluestones* when Gordon received the phone call from Carol to say she wanted to return. She and Gordon were decorating the living room. This picture of domestic harmony was quickly dissipated. Judith was told of Carol's intentions, although it was not clear to her in what capacity Carol was to return – to live with Gordon again as husband and wife, or simply to live in the family home as mother to the children. Either way, Judith believed it spelt the end of her relationship with Gordon, and she decided to go to her own home and not stay the night at *Bluestones*. Gordon's parting remark was to the effect that he would "get in touch" with her. A fairly abrupt and unceremonious dismissal of the woman who had been a constant companion and, almost certainly, a lover for some months. In his 1997 interview with the police Gordon is even more blunt – he "dumped" her, he said, when he realised Carol was returning.

Whatever words were used by Gordon to terminate his relationship with Judith, at least for the time being it seems typical of the man – cold, unemotional, manipulative. It clearly suited his purpose to have Carol back at that time and Judith was disposable. But this was not the last time that Judith was 'used' and manipulated for Gordon's purposes.

Carol's return to the matrimonial home was short-lived: Brearley puts it at a couple of days; Gordon four or five days, maybe a week. According to Gordon, Carol then announced that it wasn't working and she "didn't want to do it anymore" and she rang Brearley to come and fetch her back to Normanby. Brearley, however, says that the phone call came from Gordon, who asked him to come and fetch her as she was "going beserk".

The evidence suggests quite clearly that at this time Carol did become hysterical, smashed items of furniture and had to be restrained. What is not clear is how this situation arose. The latter part of the incident, however, was witnessed by Judith Walmsley, and indeed others.

Judith believed that her relationship with Gordon was over, and was astounded to receive a phone call from him one evening, in which he asked her to come over to the bungalow as Carol "wanted to talk" to her. Park later insisted that he made the call at Carol's behest as she wanted to talk to Judith about caring for the children once she had once more departed. The inference to be drawn is that Gordon had informed Carol at this time that his relationship with Judith was still a live issue, and that she would be living with him after Carol had departed. It was highly presumptuous of Gordon, to say the least, to believe that the woman he had summarily dismissed only a few days before would come running back to him to fill the void in his life to be left by Carol's departure. It was surely equally arrogant to assume that Judith would 'come running' at that very moment to engage in what was certain to be a very awkward situation with his estranged wife, particularly as there is nothing to suggest that Gordon had informed Judith that Carol was about to leave him again. But 'come running' she did, driving over to *Bluestones* as soon as she had received the call. One can only assume that Judith Walmsley was obsessed, or enthralled, with Gordon Park, as otherwise there seems to be no explanation as to why she should be at the beck and call of a man who had dropped her like a used rag only a day or so previously. But once again this is characteristic Gordon Park behaviour – the manipulative 'control freak' once more at work!

When Judith arrived at the Park home, she was surprised to find that the atmosphere was not tense, and the three of them sat and had a calm conversation. Carol, she says, was pleasant, announcing that she was leaving Leece again, but without the children, and she asked Judith if she would "help Gordon look after" them. Judith says that she was "astounded" at this request and gave no answer, but left the room at this point to go to the bathroom. As she was on the way back she heard raised and hysterical voices and, on re-entering the living room, she found Gordon restraining Carol on the floor. Both Gordon and Carol were shouting and Carol was kicking out violently as she was held down. Gordon shouted to Judith that she should ring "Ernie" – she knew this person to be Gordon's friend Alan Shaw. She did as requested, told Alan what was happening and he agreed to come over forthwith.

Gordon later in interview claimed that, for no reason, Carol became irrational, hysterical and violent and he was obliged to restrain her, although her violence was directed against the furniture, not him. He felt he needed assistance and asked Judith to contact Ernie. He also maintained that his father was present at one point during the incident and Alan Shaw confirms this. Before Alan and Sydney Park arrived, however, Gordon had once more dismissed Judith, telling her to leave the house, she, no doubt, having served her purpose.

Carol is restrained with the assistance of Alan Shaw, and by the time David Brearley arrives later that night she is calm. Her brief sojourn at *Bluestones* is over and she returns to Normanby-on-Tees. But not for long…

★ ★ ★

Carol's second spell on Teesside lasts probably about four months. She returns to her teaching job but she is becoming more and more depressed and unstable. That July she is referred to a consultant psychiatrist by her general practitioner and is diagnosed as suffering from a depressive illness precipitated by matrimonial disharmony. She is prescribed anti-depressants by the specialist, who believes she has "a disorganised personality in that she was unstable in her relationships". Brearley finds that she is displaying growing antagonism towards him and his son. This is manifested on one occasion when her children are staying for a week and she buys ice-cream for them but pointedly not for young Michael Brearley. Brearley realises that their relationship is failing and it comes as no great surprise to him when she announces during the school summer holidays that she was going to return for good to Leece to live with Gordon and her children. It is quite apparent to him that the decision to return is entirely motivated by her desire to be with the children, and no more than that.

In Carol's absence, Gordon and Judith have resumed their relationship. It is as if they had never parted and despite the humiliating treatment Judith had suffered at Park's hands. This time, however, it does not last and they separate by mutual agreement after four or five weeks. Judith, not surprisingly, feels insecure in the relationship and realises she does not feel the same for Gordon as she once did. There does not appear to be any great disappointment or regret on Gordon's part that their time together is over. Judith's feelings of insecurity are prescient.

The return of Carol to Leece comes about when Gordon has travelled to Normanby to pick up the children after a contact visit to their mother. He later tells the police that he finds Carol on the doorstep with her bags packed and asking to be taken to her mother's in Barrow. When they get to Leece however she decides to stay. Gordon asserts that this is a mutual decision as both of them consider it to be "worth trying again". On Carol's part it is a fateful decision…

Chapter Four

Carol and Gordon: The Endgame (1975 to 1976)

The last 11 or 12 months of the life of Carol Ann Park, at least up to the point of her death, appear to be fairly uneventful. We know that at the beginning of 1976 she is once more in a teaching job, this time at Askham School in south Cumbria. Her ability to obtain teaching posts seems, at least by today's standards, quite remarkable, particularly when one considers that she had effectively "walked out" of her last two jobs, firstly in Broughton and then in Middlesbrough.

The caretaker at the school, Grace Regan, remembers her as easy to get on with and lacking the superior and condescending attitude of some of the other teachers. She was, she says, always well-dressed and took pride in her appearance, but was quite capable of making her own clothes.

Her erstwhile lover, David Brearley, says that he was "relieved" when she had gone, despite his initial distress about her decision to leave him and return to Cumbria. He maintains that the subsequent exchanges they had over the formalities of closing bank accounts and transferring the house to his sole ownership were perfectly amicable. After that, however, he had no further contact with her, although he is destined to feature in the later police investigations into her disappearance. After her departure he fills the void in his life by taking in lodgers, until, that is, he meets the woman who will become his second wife, in late July 1976. More of that later.

It would appear that Gordon, at this time, was making efforts to restore their married life to some sort of normality. His friend and neighbour Des McWilliams says that Gordon came to his house at some point to tell him that Carol was back, and he got the impression that Gordon wanted to ensure that Carol would be received back into the community as if she had never left and would not be made to feel uncomfortable. There were no longer parties at *Bluestones* but the Parks would socialise with the McWilliams and others. Nonetheless, Desmond perceived that their relationship with each other was strained. Carol, he noticed, had lost weight and was thinner in the face.

Carol's old college friend, Rosemary Farmer, had maintained a regular correspondence with her throughout Carol's time in Normanby, and had written to her in October 1975, at Brearley's address, to invite her to her own imminent wedding. David Brearley wrote to Rosemary in turn, explaining that Carol had left him and returned to Cumbria, and it was from *Bluestones* that a letter arrived in December 1975. In that letter Carol paints a picture of contented optimism, whether that was a true reflection of her life at this time or not. She is "feeling a lot happier and more contented". Gordon, she says, "is certainly more considerate and loving and seems to have lost his aggressive nature". She tells of having recovered from a "nervous breakdown" in July that year, but is no longer on medication or visiting a psychiatrist. She speaks fondly of the children and is full of their activities. She "...could not exist without them". Gordon, she tells

Rosemary, is working hard in his second year in teaching (he is at South Newbarns Junior School in Barrow). She is looking forward to a family Christmas.

This letter is the last contact of any kind that Rosemary ever has with her friend.

Beneath this picture of domestic harmony, however, familiar tensions are brewing, and by the middle of 1976 it would appear that the Parks' marriage is once again 'heading for the rocks'. Furthermore, and although he is unaware of it at this time, Gordon later tells the police that many years later he learns that Carol in this period has, at some point, returned to old habits.

Family, and some friends of the Parks, become aware as 1976 goes on that all is not well. Ivor Price indicates that Carol has confided to his mother that there are "marital problems". Sydney Park Junior is no confidante of his brother, but on visits to *Bluestones* he detects that "things didn't appear right". He states that Carol is on medication for a nervous disorder at this time. Gordon's sister Barbara notices that Carol has changed and has become "introverted".

Kathleen Robinson, who had worked with Carol at Barrow town hall, but who had not seen her for about ten years, meets her by chance in Dalton Road in Barrow in the summer of 1976. She also notices that Carol has changed from the friendly and ebullient girl she had once known, and now seems quieter and pre-occupied. When Kathleen mentions her own marriage breakdown, Carol informs her that she too is contemplating divorce.

Anne and Derrick Walker, the owners of High Duddon guest house, had maintained some contact with Carol whilst she was in the north-east but this had ceased in the summer of 1975. They were then surprised to receive a Christmas card from her at the end of that year, the card signed "Carol and family" and the envelope bearing a Barrow postmark. Then they hear nothing more from her until they meet up at a school sports day in Ulverston in June 1976. Carol discloses that she had come back to the area "because of the children". She promises to keep in touch, but the Walkers never see or hear from Carol again.

Despite these indications of being unsettled and unhappy, there are a number of people who encounter Carol in the last few days of her life and who, by and large, find her to be forward-looking and content with her lot, and certainly giving no hint of embarking again on any life-changing move such as divorce or another affair.

Nowhere is this more evident than in the recollections of colleagues of Carol at Askam School, persons who must have been amongst the last to see her alive, other than that is Gordon and her children. The school caretaker Grace Regan can remember a conversation with Carol just before the end of term, in which Grace is invited to come to *Bluestones* during the holiday period. Carol also tells her that she is going away on holiday with Gordon and the children and that, in particular, a trip to Blackpool is planned.

A fellow teacher at the school, Neil Moffat, also recalls a conversation with Carol just before the school broke up for the summer holiday. Carol tells him "how very much she was looking forward to the new term… as she had so many things planned for the children".

William Byng, who was at that time a clerk of works and working on a construction site at the school, knew

Carol through his stepdaughter Angela Short, as Angela and her husband Malcolm were friends of the Parks. He comments that he would often see Carol at school in that summer term and she was "always cheerful and friendly". He remembers seeing Carol on the Thursday or Friday of the last week of term, and notes that she "was her usual self" and appeared to be quite untroubled.

Carol's brother Ivor, and his wife and daughter, also see Carol in the days immediately before 17 July 1976. On 15 July there is a children's dancing display at the Civic Hall in Barrow in which the Price children and also Rachel Park are involved. In a conversation with Carol in the interval, Ivor enquires of Carol as how "things are" between her and Gordon and is told that they are "not as they should be". He advises her to confide in the local vicar at Dendron church. Maureen Price and her daughter Kay also see Carol later in the week at their home. Carol seems to be in good spirits, hands over some money for a Christmas club that Maureen was running and mentions coming back to the house with a present for Kay, whose birthday would have been on Sunday 18 July. This visit, it seems, must have been on Friday 16 July. Carol, however, does not return with a present and the Prices never see her again.

The Park's friend and neighbour Des McWilliams also has a conversation with Carol "a day or a couple of days" before her disappearance. Carol had been consulting him about the possibility of tracing her natural parents, something which, Des recalls, Gordon appeared to support. In this last discussion Carol indicates that she intends to go ahead in an attempt to find her birth parents and Des agrees she should as it was clearly something that was "so important to her". On the face of it this was not an issue that was a bone of contention between Gordon and Carol.

Another neighbour, Mary Robinson, recalls that the last time she saw Carol was "shortly after the schools broke up for the summer holidays in 1976". It is quite possible that the term actually ended on the Thursday rather than Friday 16 July, so this cannot necessarily be taken as an indication that Mary saw Carol on or after 17 July. Indeed, she remembers that Carol expressed relief at the "the holidays coming round" and she got the impression that "the Parks were getting ready to go off on holiday somewhere". Mary, too, never sees Carol again.

An interesting and slightly different picture is painted by Susan Dalton. Susan had been employed at Dunlop House children's home when Vanessa had been resident there before she was adopted by the Parks, and had also been briefly employed later by Carol and Gordon in 1971 as a "nanny". After this she had remained in touch with Carol, knew about the Brearley episode and was conscious in 1975 that Carol "was not as happy as she used to be". Susan cannot recall the timing of her last meeting with Carol, but remembers that she was told that "Gordon wanted to go off for the day with the kids but she didn't want to as it was the day after finishing school". This would tend to suggest that the trip to Blackpool on 17 July was a pre-planned event. Susan is quite emphatic that Carol loved her children "dearly" and that, if she did leave her marriage, she would never have not kept in contact with them.

As far as Gordon himself is concerned, when interviewed by the police in 1997 he maintained that his relationship with Carol at this time was "working". It was not "wonderful" but there were, he said, no major arguments and he was not aware of any "men friends". In 2004, however, he told the interviewing officers that he was now better informed. He had been told that she had in the period in question been "associating with" men, and he gave two names with which he had been since provided – a solicitor called Nuttall, and a police officer called McBride. The names are familiar to the writer. Gordon Nuttall was a solicitor in Barrow, who much later became a district judge; and there was a detective constable called McBride with Barrow police. Park emphasises, however, that he cannot recall the source of his information and that it was "hearsay and tittle-tattle". There may too have been others, he says, but he did not have, and had no reason to have, in 1976 any suspicions that Carol was engaged in affairs with other men.

There is indeed no evidence that Carol was having extra-marital relationships at this time with men in general and the persons named in particular. The absence of evidence, however, does not mean that she was not treading the same well-worn path that she had followed in earlier years. It seems almost beyond question that Carol had great difficulty in remaining faithful to her marriage vows, that she slipped easily into relationships with other men and that she displayed what was close to an addiction with adultery. Despite her obvious very strong love for and attachment to her children, she had demonstrated in the past an apparent readiness to jeopardise her relationship with them for the sake of an affair with another man.

In short it would not be at all surprising if Carol Park was actively pursuing other relationships during the last 12 months of her marriage to Gordon. It would perhaps

A Very Cumbrian Murder

not be an overstatement to say that it would be surprising if she was not.

It is surely disingenuous of Gordon to claim that he had no "suspicions" at this time that Carol was once again having an affair or affairs. Given Carol's 'track record' over the previous two years, in which she had engaged in two major extra-marital relationships, both of which he knew about, he would have to have been extraordinarily naïve to have convinced himself that his wife was a 'reformed' character and was not going to 'stray' again. Naïve he clearly was not!

If there were such affairs at this time, it seems highly likely that Gordon's state of awareness would have gone beyond mere suspicion. Carol did not have the luxury then of periods away from home at college or summer schools. She would have had to conduct her liaisons whilst holding down a full-time job, running a household and looking after three young children. It seems unlikely that, in these circumstances, her activities would have escaped the notice of a husband who was only too familiar with her propensities?

There would, of course, have had to have been a motive for the act of unspeakable violence that was shortly to be committed against Carol Park. Perhaps one illicit relationship too many? The 'straw that broke the camel's back'?

What impression would outsiders have had of the Park menage mid-way through July 1976, and in particular of the marriage itself? There were clearly some who realised all was not well in the relationship, but, at the same time, there were plenty of others who would have believed that Carol and Gordon were 'rubbing along' satisfactorily, and even some who saw in Carol's continuing cheerful and sunny disposition cause for optimism. There were none surely who could have anticipated in their wildest dreams the cataclysmic event that was about to engulf the family, even if they did not learn the true nature of that event for more than 20 years. Nor is it likely that any of them would have predicted that within days Carol would have seemingly disappeared from the face of the earth.

★ ★ ★

Either Friday 16 July or Saturday 17 July 1976 was almost certainly the last day of Carol Park's life. As to what transpired on the later of those two days, there is almost no evidence, beyond the obviously self-serving account later provided by Gordon to the police. The eldest of the three children, Vanessa, was only eight years of age at this time and her recollection of that day is virtually non-existent. She can remember a trip to Blackpool but cannot recall where it falls into the general sequence of events, and cannot assist as to what happened during the trip or indeed during the entire day. She simply remembers that there was a time when her mother "just wasn't there". She seems to think there was another man in Carol's life at this time but she may well be confusing this with the earlier occasion she had 'disappeared' and was living with David Brearley, or merely shared the assumption made by Gordon, that she had left for another man. Vanessa seems to think that Carol had on this last occasion taken no clothes with her. It is difficult to know, however, how much reliance can be put on this belief. What she does say is that there was no real discussion with her father or with the other children as to why her mother was no longer there, either at this time or later.

Jeremy was six at the time and remembers a trip to Blackpool with his father and sisters and without his mother. He had a "notion" that his father was "sad" during the outing. He remembers coming home and thinks the "wardrobes were empty", and recalls sitting on the bed in his parents' bedroom with Gordon and the girls and his father telling them that their mother had "left home and wouldn't be coming back". Although this appears to correspond with what may have happened on Saturday 17 July 1976, Jeremy cannot place the events in any particular time-frame and again may be confusing this occasion with the earlier 'disappearance'.

Rachel was only five years of age and basically has no memory at all of the time when her mother was no longer around.

Gordon, as one might expect, has a much clearer recollection of events, even when interviewed about them in 1997 and again in 2004. He said it had been a decision made in advance to go to Blackpool that Saturday, a decision in which Carol would have participated. It was intended to be a special treat for the children – he himself "hated the place". On the morning, he stated, Carol didn't want to go. He could not remember why this was, but didn't believe it was that she was ill. There was no argument over her decision – as far as he was concerned she was a "hard-working woman" and if she wanted to stay at home that was alright with him. When they left *Bluestones* she was still in bed. He could not remember whether the children would have seen her that morning but there was no reason why they would not have done.

He went on to tell the interviewing officers that when they returned home later that day, Carol had gone. His first thoughts were "here we go again". She had removed her rings and left them on the dressing-table (these had been recovered by the police in September 1976). Gordon said he regarded this as a "statement of intent" – she was saying "I'm leaving, goodbye". His recollection was that some of her clothing had gone and some of her personal jewellery. He didn't know now whether she had taken any house keys with her. There was no evidence of a break-in and no blood in the bed or house or any sign of a struggle.

It is worth mentioning at this point that Gordon Park was interviewed by police in 1976, when obviously his memory of the events of 17 July would have been much clearer than they were 21 or even 28 years later. The file of evidence that had been gathered in 1976 by the police, however, had 'gone missing' (more of this later) and Gordon was made aware of this when he was interviewed in 1997. He was able to use this to his advantage, and indeed 'milked' the situation of the 'missing file' throughout the interviews. If his memory was fallible in 1997 or 2004, he could refer the interviewers to "what I said in 1976", knowing full well that the officers could not refer to those earlier replies. For this reason, it was almost impossible to point to any inconsistencies in his evidence – his stock reply when pressed on any point would be "I'm not certain now, but I would have been more so in 1976"! It was a situation which undoubtedly hampered the police in the interviews in 1997 and 2004.

What is certain is that Gordon did not report his wife's 'disappearance' immediately after 17 July 1976, and it was not until early September that the police were made aware that she had left the marital home. For Gordon, however, there was no reason to raise the alarm at this early stage – she had left home before, he said, now she had done it again, and there was no reason to believe that she was in any danger or had come to any harm.

There is one other certainty, however: Carol Ann Park was brutally murdered, and it has to be the case that the crime was committed on either 16 or 17 July 1976, because since that latter date there is no evidence of any kind that she was still alive…

Chapter Five

Missing Person Enquiry: 1976

Between 17 July and 4 September 1976, by his own admission, Gordon Park made no attempt to locate his wife. He did not contact David Brearley or any other of her previous 'lovers', known or suspected. He did not contact the Price family to ascertain if any of them had heard from Carol. His lack of 'enquiry' seems strange when one considers that on previous occasions when Carol had been absent from home she had always kept in touch with her children and family. It is not strange at all, of course, when we know that Gordon knew she would not be making contact with anyone ever again!

Gordon could not, however, completely avoid keeping Carol's absence to himself. There were encounters with others where he was more or less obliged to disclose or explain her disappearance. There was for example a visit to his father and the latter's new wife in late July (Park Senior and Gordon's mother had by now divorced and his father had married Hazel Butters in October 1975, a lady he had known for some years previously). Mrs Park recalls that Gordon arrived at their home in company with the three children but without Carol who, he said, had "gone missing". He went on to explain that he and the children had departed on a trip to Blackpool, leaving Carol "ill" in bed, and that, on their return, there was no sign of her, although her belongings were still in the house. Hazel and Sidney, however, both believed that Carol had simply "left" her husband once again.

Des McWilliams was told by Gordon that Carol had left again, but apparently "without taking anything with her". Des says Gordon was angry and concerned but also "mystified" by Carol's latest disappearance.

On the first Sunday of the school holidays (this must have been 18 July) Gordon's old school friend and erstwhile sailing companion Malcolm Short made an unannounced visit to *Bluestones* with his wife. The Shorts had left the Furness area in 1969 and made only occasional return trips to Barrow. The visit to the Park home was quite bizarre. They met Gordon outside the house, there was no sign of the children according to Malcolm, they were not invited into the bungalow and, after about 15 minutes, they decided to leave. When the Shorts asked after Carol, they were told by Gordon that she had "gone" and that he believed that she had 'walked out' on him. He appeared to be annoyed by Carol's disappearance. Mrs Short recalls that they were told that Carol hadn't taken anything with her, not even her purse, something which Angela Short regarded as very strange.

Given that the Shorts were very old friends and that they and the Parks saw each other only very rarely, the lack of an invitation to come into the house seems strange indeed. But again, perhaps not, when one considers that there may well have been things inside that Gordon wished to keep hidden – blood or other evidence of a brutal murder, perhaps? The absence of the children may also be indicative. If, as seems highly likely, Carol had been killed in the home, and as recently as a day or two before, there must have been a significant amount of 'tidying up' that needed to be done.

Gordon's brother and sister also learnt during the school holidays, either from Gordon directly or through their mother, that Carol had "gone off again". Barbara is told by her mother that Carol had not gone on the Blackpool trip because she was feeling unwell and had not been seen again.

As the summer went on, of course, the time approached when the new school term was due to start and Carol would have been expected to return to her teaching duties. Gordon would surely have been aware of this but, if he needed any reminder, he would have got it when one of Carol's teaching colleagues, Marion Lesley, rang *Bluestones* on 31 August with a view to informing Carol that a staff meeting was to take place the following day. She was informed, presumably by Gordon, that Carol had "left home".

By 4 September 1976, therefore, a small number of people had been made aware that Carol was no longer living at home – a few friends, Carol's work colleagues, and Gordon's, but not Carol's, family. But the message they were getting was that Carol had left home voluntarily and of her own accord, there was nothing sinister about her absence and there was no cause for concern for her welfare. In particular, there was no need to alert or notify the 'authorities'. However, on that date, exactly seven weeks after Carol's 'disappearance', and probably two days before the new school term was due to start, Gordon suddenly decided to change tack, and reported her absence to the police…

★ ★ ★

When interviewed by the police in 1997, Gordon said that, as the new school term loomed, he became "concerned" when Carol did not come home in order to prepare for her return to school. He thereupon decided to contact, not the police, but his solicitors. His conduct does not seem at all consistent with that of an 'innocent' man. If he had not murdered his wife, and genuinely believed that she had left him for another man, then it must surely have dawned on him long before 4 September that there was more to it than that. Carol may have had her own bank account but she would have had only a limited amount of money. She would have had no clothes beyond those she was wearing when she had left home. But far more significantly, she, a doting mother, had made no attempt whatsoever to contact her children. It would surely have been abundantly clear after a few days, let alone seven weeks, that there was something amiss and that her absence couldn't simply be dismissed as desertion. Gordon himself later accepted that his failure to report her disappearance for such a long period could be seen as suspicious and it would have been "better" if he had brought it to the attention of the police after "two days".

Then there is the very strange and quite irrational decision to seek legal advice as the first option rather than to go directly to the police. Gordon never really explains why he took this course, and neither is he entirely clear about what advice he was given by his solicitor, although he believes it "would have been" to report Carol's disappearance to the police. He is of course being interviewed here more than 20 years after the event, and he is playing the '1976 card' for all it's worth – ie. that he would have given a cogent and accurate account when he was interviewed then, and if the police hadn't lost the file they would know what he had said!

The reality of course is that Gordon Park could not report his wife as 'missing' in those early days after her disappearance. He needed to cover his tracks, to dispose of the body, if he had not already done so, and destroy the evidence of a brutal murder in his home. To have allowed the police into *Bluestones* at an early stage would have been a recipe for disaster. By the same token, he could not have delayed his subsequent actions for any longer than he did: whilst the school may have been aware that Carol had "left home", her work colleagues would still have been expecting her to return to her teaching duties at the start of term, and when she failed to appear it would have been inevitable that 'questions' would have been asked. Gordon needed to act to prevent this happening. To have gone to his solicitors rather than the police, however, is really inexplicable and a course of action that would come back to haunt him.

It is in fact Park's solicitor who contacts the police. Ex-PC Alexander Millar recalls that he received a telephone call at Dalton police station one summer afternoon from a solicitor who informed him that "a Mr Park" wanted to report his wife as missing from home. The solicitor in question would no doubt have been from Messrs Forresters, the firm that Gordon says he visited in order to seek advice about Carol's disappearance. Mr Millar recalls that the solicitor told him that Mrs Park had been missing for "three weeks". We do not know if this is the information the solicitor had been given by Park, but, bearing in mind that Mr Millar is trying to remember events that occurred some than 21 years previously, it is quite possible he is mistaken about this. It is fair to say that he believes the call was in "July"; furthermore, the official Missing Person form, completed on 4 September 1976, does record the last sighting of Carol Park as being

17 July. This form, which appears to have been the only document to have survived from the 1976 investigation, was sent to and retained by the Missing Persons Bureau at New Scotland Yard. It was completed, not by ex-PC Millar, but by a PC Shepherd, who was deceased by the time of the 1997 investigation. The form refers to Gordon Park as the "informant" and is timed at 4.15 pm on 4 September, so presumably it would have been completed sometime later on the day that Mr Millar receives the phone call, and in a face-to-face interview with Gordon by PC Shepherd.

Gordon had also clearly decided that it was politic at this time to break the news of Carol's disappearance to her family. Ivor Price receives a visit from Gordon on a Saturday morning in early September 1976 – this would almost certainly be 4 September. Gordon tells him he has some "bad news" and goes on to relate that Carol "had gone missing" at least six weeks previously. According to Ivor, Gordon told him that the last time he had seen Carol was when he left her in bed, as she was unwell, prior to the rest of the family departing for a day out in Blackpool. Gordon later denied that he had told Ivor that Carol had reported feeling unwell. Ivor, not surprisingly, is annoyed that Gordon had not brought this news to him before this time and that he had delayed for so long in reporting her missing. He is clearly alarmed as on the previous occasion Carol had been away from home she had kept her family informed of her whereabouts. It would seem that this visit to Ivor is on the same day as, but before, Gordon's contact with the solicitors and the later phone call to the police. It is understandable, of course, why Gordon would not have wanted to alert the Prices to Carol's disappearance much before this, as they may well have been suspicious about her lack of communication and may have wanted the matter to be referred to the police before Gordon felt himself ready to bring the matter to their attention.

* * *

On 4 September 1976, the police investigation that began in connection with Carol Park was a Missing Person enquiry. We do not know, however, what the scope of that investigation was, what evidence was gathered or whether it ever became more than just a Missing Person enquiry and metamorphosed into a criminal investigation. We cannot be entirely sure which witnesses were interviewed or what they said when interviewed. We cannot be sure either how widely the search for Carol was conducted or over what period of time. We know that Gordon Park was interviewed by police officers, but we do not know whether he was treated as a witness or, indeed, interviewed under caution as a potential suspect in a murder case. We do not know what conclusions the investigators formed as to what had happened to Carol.

The principal reason for this almost total lack of information was the fact that the file of evidence gathered in the enquiry had, by August 1997, mysteriously disappeared. I say 'mysteriously' because the 'file' in question would not have been a few sheets of paper, but a very substantial volume of evidence, and not something that could easily have been 'mislaid'. Given that it was an enquiry in which, almost inevitably, experienced police officers would have at some point concluded that Carol Park was no longer alive and that 'foul play' may well have been involved in her disappearance, it would have been very important that the file of evidence should have been carefully preserved and stored. In 1976, of course, there would have been no data stored on a computer – the 'file' would have been purely a 'paper' one, and a sizeable one at that. It is difficult not to come to the conclusion that its disappearance is either sinister or the result of gross incompetence.

In 1997 and thereafter, as one might expect, various conspiracy theories were hatched as to why the file had disappeared. One in particular was that, as the main beneficiary of the missing file was Gordon Park, it had been "destroyed" by senior officers as part of some Freemasonic 'cover-up' enterprise. The presence of Freemasonry in the police service was no doubt more widespread and less transparent in 1976 than in more recent times, but the fatal flaw in this theory is that there is no evidence whatsoever that Gordon Park himself was a Freemason! The more likely explanation perhaps is that police files are not routinely kept in perpetuity; there is a 'weeding' process, and that, although this file should have been preserved, it was mistakenly destroyed at some stage as part of this process. Incompetent but not sinister.

Another difficulty faced by the investigators in the 1997 murder investigation, and this was a full-blown murder investigation now, was that many of the police officers who were involved in the 1976 enquiry, and who might have been able to provide some of the information about the scope and results of that enquiry, were by that time either dead or retired and now unable or unwilling to share their recollections. In particular, the two senior detectives who had led the enquiry and who had interviewed Park were now deceased.

Furthermore, of the persons who may have been interviewed as material witnesses in 1976, many were now either deceased or elderly, and if they were still alive, were not necessarily able to recall with any clarity events that occurred more than 20 years previously. Again, where witnesses were re-interviewed in 1997, one could not be at all sure that what they were saying at that time was the same as they were saying in 1976.

There is no doubt that the missing file was to cause the 1997 investigators great difficulties, not least because, as we have seen already, they were on the back foot in interviewing Gordon Park, who was able, again and again, to manipulate the interrogation by claiming that his memory of events was lacking now but the accurate answer to their questions was to be found in the 1976 interviews. Park, of course, was soon aware that the 1976 interviews were lost and he played on this adeptly throughout the interviews in 1997 and 2004. This meant that the officers interviewing him were not able to catch him in any inconsistencies in his accounts.

★ ★ ★

In the 1997 investigation there were only half-a-dozen ex-police officers who were able to contribute anything to that enquiry as to what had transpired in 1976, and the sum total of their recollections did not amount to very much. Those who were central to the 1976 enquiry were either dead by 1997, or, as indicated previously, either unwilling or unable to assist.

Ex-PC Millar, who took the original phone call from Forresters solicitors, did visit *Bluestones* the same afternoon and spoke with Gordon. He recalls, almost certainly mistakenly, that Gordon said his wife had been missing for three weeks. The house and outbuildings were searched. Mr Millar also recalls being told by Gordon that Carol had not taken any clothes or money with her, and that she had left home on previous occasions. He cannot recall whether the children were present at this time or if there was a boat to be seen in the garden.

William Lawson, who retired in 1984, was in 1976 a police sergeant stationed at Dalton-in-Furness, and was involved to some extent in the Missing Person enquiry. He recalls visiting *Bluestones* on two or three occasions. On one occasion he got the impression that Gordon did not want him to enter the bungalow and their conversation took place on the front doorstep; he also formed the impression that Park did not want him to interview the children, who, he was told, were not at home. Mr Lawson searched the local fields on several occasions, but cannot recall whether there was a search of Leece tarn. He was not involved much further than this in the enquiry, which was taken over by CID officers.

Mr Lawson, however, was aware that Carol had not withdrawn any money from any bank accounts following her disappearance on this occasion, that no clothes had been taken by her and that on previous occasions when away from home she had kept in touch with her family. Her details, he knew, had been circulated to DHSS offices nationwide with a negative result. The general consensus amongst himself and his colleagues, said Mr Lawson, was that, given the above facts, some harm had befallen Mrs Park and that Gordon should have been "taken into a police station for questioning". (He was questioned of course, but in what circumstances and whether this was following an arrest is by no means certain).

Another retired officer, ex-Police Sergeant John Wilson, was working at Ulverston police station in 1976, and was also a police liaison officer for the Furness Mountain Rescue Team. He recalls, as part of the enquiry, arranging a search of old mine shafts in the Furness area.

Other than looking down old mine shafts and searching fields, and circulating her details, it is not known exactly what steps the police took in 1976 to try to locate Carol Park. One imagines that 'dragging' Leece tarn was a 'given', and there is some suggestion that the garden at *Bluestones* was dug up. Almost certainly the Mountain Rescue teams in the locality and south Cumbria would have played a part, searching beaches, woods and the Coniston fells, and perhaps further afield. The most obvious places to dispose of a body in the Lake District? The clue is in the title, but sending frogmen down into the depths of the dozens of lakes and meres in the county would be like looking for the proverbial needle in the haystack. One has only to look at the period of time it took for Donald Campbell's body to be recovered (34 years) and the failure of the initial attempts to find him in Coniston Water, despite the fact that there was at least a reasonable idea of his body's location.

One CID officer who was involved in the enquiry, but not until he moved to Ulverston CID from Barrow CID in late 1976, was ex-Detective Constable Colin Towers. He acknowledges, as do other officers, that his memory of the events of 1976 is vague and sketchy. He confirms, however, that the investigation revealed that Carol had withdrawn no money from any bank account after 17 July. He has a firm recollection that officers involved in the enquiry were, to a man, convinced that Carol was dead. He remembers going to Gordon's home in the company of Detective Sergeant Johnson on more than one occasion but cannot recall if they went inside, spoke to the children or what local searches for Carol were carried out. He was aware that Carol's details were circulated to every other police force in the country.

Mr Towers does not recall if Park was ever confronted as a suspect, but then he was not involved in the major part of the enquiry, which he believed was undertaken by DS Johnson. He remarks that the Missing Person file became quite substantial as time went on, and occasionally the then-Detective Inspector Maurice Wilkinson would generate further enquiries on the matter. The "Misper" file, he says, was accessible in those days at either Barrow or Ulverston police station. One interesting comment he makes is that it is his memory that Park never contacted the police to ascertain the progress of the enquiry, and that "it always appeared that we had to approach him".

There seems little doubt that the police investigators in 1976 must have come to, and did come to, the conclusion that Carol Park was dead. Everything pointed to this conclusion. No-one had seen her alive since 17 July and there were no sightings of or traces of her existence anywhere in the country. She had taken no clothes and had withdrawn no money. She had failed to return to a job which she loved. She had made no attempt to contact either her children or her wider family. She seemed to have disappeared off the face of the earth. Unlike other celebrated 'disappearing acts' she lacked completely their advantages. She was no Lord Lucan, who could perhaps rely on rich, aristocratic friends to assist or facilitate his 'disappearance'. Neither, like a Ronnie Biggs, did she have access to large sums of money which could be defrayed to change her appearance or to arrange a new life abroad. The obvious and irresistible inference was that Carol Park was no more…

★ ★ ★

If the investigators in 1976, as they almost certainly did, believed that Carol Park was dead, it was no great quantum leap for them to go on and believe that she had been murdered and her body disposed of. If she had taken her own life, or had died as a result of accident or misadventure, then she would surely have been quickly found or there would have been evidence of how and where she had met her end. One imagines that the experienced officers who led the 1976 enquiry would not have failed to come to this conclusion. Furthermore, given the history of the Park marriage and Gordon's conduct after Carol's disappearance, it would seem equally likely that they would see him as the prime suspect.

We do not, however, know what view was taken by the 'leads' in the investigation. Ex-Detective Sergeant Johnson, although still alive in 1997 I believe, was unable to assist those officers undertaking the murder enquiry in that year. The senior officers who seem to have been those interviewing Gordon Park in 1976, Maurice Wilkinson and Innes Williams, were by 1997 both deceased. We do, however, have a hint of what view the latter took, by virtue of Gordon's remark in the 2004 interviews that Mr Williams had told him he "was number one suspect".

Could the police in 1976 have gone beyond their suspicions and beliefs and actually charged Gordon Park at that time with the murder of his wife? The answer is 'no', because the available evidence then was a long way short of providing any prospect of his being convicted of such a crime.

The main difficulty in 1976, of course, was that there was no body. The absence of a body is not a bar to a charge of murder, and there have been cases over the years where persons have been convicted of murder in just such situations. A case in question, in which I had some involvement, was that of Hassan Shatanawi, who was convicted of the murder of his wife following a trial at Newcastle Crown Court in 1994. Her body was never found but there was strong circumstantial evidence that she was dead, had been murdered, and, indeed, murdered by her husband. There are some parallels with the situation facing the Carol Park officers in 1976 in that there was probably sufficient evidence to say that she was dead and had been unlawfully killed; what was lacking, however, was any cogent evidence that Gordon Park was the killer or, indeed, had any connection with her disappearance. There was no forensic evidence, no 'smoking gun', no confessions, no false alibi, no eye-witnesses – or certainly as far as we are aware, in the absence of the "Misper" file.

Charging Park with murder in 1976 was therefore a 'non-starter'. There was, furthermore, one piece of evidence, it seems, in 1976 which if anything appeared at first glance to cast doubt on Gordon's guilt. This was the evidence of Sabrine Dixon.

It is known that Mrs Dixon provided information to the investigators in 1976, but of course there was by 1997 no permanent record of what she might have said. It seems likely, however, that in broad terms what she told police in 1976 was much the same as the written evidence she provided in 1997.

Sabrine Dixon, in July 1976, was the Parks' next door neighbour in Leece. She told the police that on "the day that Carol disappeared", at about 11.00 am she was working in her kitchen, when she saw a pale blue

Volkswagen Beetle "pull up at *Bluestones*". The car remained in its stationary position "for about 20-30 minutes" before driving off. She thought the driver was a man of about Gordon's age. She also thought she had seen the Beetle parked at the bungalow on a couple of previous occasions. On this particular occasion, she said, she knew that the family had gone to Blackpool or Morecambe for the day, and she thought that this included Carol.

Taken at face value, this was clearly a very important piece of evidence. It was something that Gordon said he was aware of in 1976, and he had recruited Mrs Dixon as a potential witness should he ever be required to satisfy a court of his innocence.

It goes without saying that the police investigators in 1976 would have made inquiries to establish the identity of the blue VW Beetle and of its owner. We do not know the results of those inquiries, but inquiries were made again in 1997 and, no doubt, with the same people and with the same result.

One person from Carol's past who owned, or had owned, a VW Beetle, was John Wilkes, who used to give Carol lifts to school when she worked in Broughton-in-Furness. He would collect her from *Bluestones* and would sometimes drive up the drive to the bungalow. He owned the vehicle until "sometime after 1975". It seems highly unlikely, however, that this is the vehicle in question. In the first place, Wilkes says the car was bright orange. Secondly, the need for him to go to Carol's home to pick her up had long passed by July 1976, and there is no evidence that he ever went to Leece in the car after this time or, indeed, went to *Bluestones* in any circumstances after this time.

A Very Cumbrian Murder

Marjorie Mantle did not live in Leece, but she was a regular visitor to a house called Holmstead, which was actually at the back of the Park's property. This cottage was occupied until the early 1970s by her sister Cicely Reeves, and then, until the 1980s by her niece Susan. Mrs Mantle purchased a dark blue VW Beetle in the mid-1970s and would drive the car to Leece, remaining at Holmstead for any time between 15 minutes and an hour and a half. She did not, however, know the Parks, and had never had any contact with them, and there seems no reason why she should ever park on their drive.

During their inquiries, either firstly in 1976 or in 1997, the police traced another person in Barrow who would have owned a blue VW Beetle at this time. Mary Robinson, not the Mary Robinson who was the Park's neighbour, drove such a car regularly and her daughter and her two sons would have driven it also from time to time. But that is really where the story ends as the family had no obvious connection with Leece, and the only slight connection with the Parks is that Mary's daughter Margaret may have been at school with Gordon's sister Barbara, and the latter was a bridesmaid, along with Margaret, at the wedding of one of her sons. Again, however, there seems no conceivable reason why this vehicle should have been at *Bluestones* on 17 July 1976.

Gordon Park had a work colleague at South Newbarns Junior School called Colin Smith. Colin was also the owner of a VW Beetle at the material time. Again, however, it seems highly unlikely that this was the mysterious vehicle seen by Mrs Dixon. In the first place the car was red, not blue. Secondly, according to Colin Smith, he didn't really become a close friend of Gordon until a time after Carol's final disappearance and so had no reason to go Gordon's home until then. Neither does he seem to have ever known Carol.

It was inevitable that the police enquiry in 1976 would include interviewing Carol's erstwhile lover David Brearley and ascertaining what, if any, vehicles he owned in July 1976. According to Brearley, he owned a sky-blue K-registered Ford Escort at this time and no doubt the police would have checked the details he provided as to the car and the period of his ownership. A Ford Escort of course is not a VW Beetle or even close, and Brearley appears to have had at least a partial alibi for 17 July and other pre-occupations at this time (see later).

Sabrine Dixon herself, when seen for a second time in 1997, was somewhat less certain about her sighting. The reason, she said, that she linked the VW Beetle to the Blackpool trip and Carol going missing was that it was "unusual for nobody to be at *Bluestones*". This is clearly a misconceived observation, since, during term-time, the bungalow would be unoccupied for most of the day! When pressed, Mrs Dixon concedes that she doesn't "remember" how it was she knew the day was the day the family went to Blackpool.

It is interesting that Vanessa Park comments that the drive to *Bluestones* looked rather like a lane, and that it was not uncommon for cars to drive up it. Colin Smith also observes that it was difficult for cars to park on the road outside the bungalow.

The evidence of the sighting of the mysterious blue car was certainly taken seriously by the investigators in 1997, as it would almost certainly be in 1976. It also caused some concern for my colleagues and me in 1997. It is fair to say, however, that the evidence, when subjected to careful scrutiny, seemed quite inconsequential and ultimately was largely discounted as having any significant bearing on the case. Even taken at face value, the occupant of the vehicle was not seen to leave the bungalow with any person, dead or alive, and he or she was not inside the property long enough to carry out a brutal murder and dispose of the body and arrange the scene so as to leave no trace of the deed. All in all it seems very plain that the 'blue Beetle' was a 'red herring'…

Chapter Six

Gordon: Two Divorces and Two Weddings
(1976 to 1997)

After Carol's final 'disappearance', and despite the fact that from 4 September 1976 she was being treated as a "missing person", life went on in the Park household and, it seemed, on a fairly even keel. Vanessa recalls that the family "never spoke" about what had happened. According to her, Gordon "made a real effort" with the children, reading to them and engaging with their hobbies and interests. She was aware that her mother's clothes were still in her parents' bedroom, although the three children were not allowed to enter. Eventually, she says, she realised that her father had sorted them into boxes and put them in the attic. At Gordon's suggestion, all three children wrote letters to their mother to inform her of what and how they were doing – these were given to and retained by Gordon. Other than this it appears that Carol had been 'airbrushed' out of the family's life.

Jeremy has few memories of this initial period after his mother had gone, although he recalls being happy at home, but less so at school – he was now at South Newbarns School, where his father taught, and his education was disrupted by his being moved from class to class to avoid Gordon having to teach him. He remembers in this period, however, that his father had one or two girlfriends, and recalls one called Pam and another called Pat, neither of whom were on the scene for very long.

Rachel, the youngest child, was only five years old when her mother departed from her life, but she also recalls that Carol was seldom mentioned. She does however remember odd occasions in her later years when Gordon would make brief references to her mother – one being when she attained some O-level passes and her father remarked that her mother would have been proud of her. She noted that on these few occasions that he did bring Carol up in conversation, that he was "pensive in a sad kind of way".

Vanessa felt that during this time her father discouraged contact with the Prices, but she herself would seek them out and became much closer to her uncle Ivor and her maternal grandmother. Ivor says that in these years he and his wife rarely saw Gordon, and then only at family occasions such as weddings and funerals. Nonetheless, he does allude to one occasion when, in about 1977, he and his daughter and the Park children went sailing with Gordon on Windermere, in a large dinghy with an open top.

Maureen Price, on the other hand, felt that Gordon became friendlier during this period. She would, however, out of necessity, have had more contact with Gordon, as she frequently helped out with his young children, particularly by often picking them up from school. Her perception was that life at *Bluestones* was going on "as normal". Another illustration of this was that the younger Price children would continue to go to Leece and play with their cousins, and Kay, the middle daughter, recalls sailing trips with Gordon in a wooden dinghy on one of the lakes in the southern Lake District.

The experience of friends and neighbours following Carol's final disappearance was much the same as that of the children – life went on as normal, but Carol was never or rarely mentioned. Carol's college friend, Rosemary Farmer, had had no communication from her since December 1975, and then was surprised to receive a telephone call from the police in late 1976, the officer asking if Rosemary had been in touch with Carol recently. Following this call, Rosemary rang *Bluestones* and spoke initially to Gordon, who, she says, was calm and quite "matter of fact" about Carol's disappearance, giving the impression that he believed Carol had left home again "to start a new life". To Rosemary's surprise, Gordon did not remain on the phone for long before passing her on to the children. From that point Rosemary's contact with the family was only very occasional, and in her rare telephone calls to the Park household, Gordon, she says, never raised the issue of "Carol" and when she inquired if Gordon had heard anything from her or about her he was, she says, "very dismissive". Gordon did once ring her much later to tell her that Vanessa was pregnant, but, apart from that, she heard nothing further from the family of her old friend.

The Parks' neighbour Mary Robinson observed that nothing much changed at *Bluestones* – Gordon went on with his life and bringing up the children, who appeared to be normal and healthy. Gordon, however, "never spoke about Carol after she'd gone".

Des McWilliams was quite convinced that Gordon could not have done Carol any "deliberate harm" and he remained friends with him, continuing to visit *Bluestones* regularly. Nevertheless, he avoided raising the subject of Carol with Gordon, who never raised the subject himself.

Rosemary Hadwin was Gordon's stepsister, her mother having married Gordon's father in 1975 after his divorce from Gordon's mother. She recalls that her mother was often called upon to look after the Park children after Carol had gone. She also recalls, interestingly, that in 1977 or 1978 Gordon brought a lady called Judith Walmsley to tea at the Senior Parks' home. She wasn't sure of the status of their relationship at the time, but she maintains that Gordon "stopped seeing Judith at some stage in the late seventies".

Rosemary's mother, Hazel, also says that at Christmas 1977, 18 months after Carol's disappearance, Gordon introduced her husband and herself to a "lady friend" called Judith Walmsley, although their relationship did not "become serious".

Both Gordon and Judith, of course, claim that their 'relationship' had ceased to exist well before Carol had left the scene. It is difficult to see, however, why Gordon's relations should be untruthful about this matter, and if Judith was still part of his life in July 1976, then this factor may have provided a motive in Carol's murder. Gordon is certainly very emphatic in his police interviews in his claims that Judith was "history" by the time of Carol's disappearance. On the other hand, the evidence tends to suggest that their "relationship" was never very profound, and that Judith was perhaps never more than a convenient friend and possible babysitter.

Some of Gordon's colleagues at South Newbarns School played a part, to a lesser or greater extent, in his life in the months and years immediately following Carol's disappearance. A fellow teacher, Elizabeth Hull, babysat for Gordon on one occasion. She recalls that Gordon was very depressed but flung himself into his teaching and extra-curricular activities. Elizabeth never asked Gordon about what might have happened to Carol, but she remembers being in the company of others when the matter was raised and Gordon commenting, in a tone of disbelief, that he was "under suspicion" and that he was anticipating that the police would be digging up his garden.

Sheila Edmonds was a dinner supervisor at the school and, like Gordon, had become a 'single parent'. In her case, her husband had walked out abruptly and without warning, and, as a result, she saw nothing strange in the reported manner of Carol's departure. She became friendly with Gordon when he began to attend meetings of the local Gingerbread group. This was a sort of social group for single parents and their families, and Sheila was already a member when Gordon joined. She remembers Gordon "dating" a woman from the group called Pam Baines, although this did not become a more permanent relationship, and in time Gordon formed a more serious liaison with another member, Cath Sillars. Sheila also helped Gordon by babysitting on several occasions.

It was during this period that Gordon forged a close friendship with another teaching colleague, Colin Smith. Colin had started at South Newbarns School only in September 1975, and initially had no social contact with Gordon. It was through Gordon, however, that he met Gordon's mother Elsie, and through Elsie that he joined the Elizabethan Players amateur dramatic group in Barrow. It was, however, through their mutual interest in sailing that the friendship of the two men developed from the summer of 1976. In May and June 1976 both attended a course at the Tower Wood Centre on Lake Windermere, a course which was designed to qualify teachers and youth leaders to instruct pupils and young persons in the rudiments of sailing. Gordon of course was already a proficient and experienced sailor and it is no surprise that on the course he gained an 'advanced certificate', which in effect qualified him to instruct in all aspects of dinghy sailing on inland waters, including boat handling, boat maintenance, knot tying and other skills. Colin attained a lesser qualification, which meant he could only teach sailing skills to children if he was accompanied by another teacher.

From this point, Colin and Gordon became regular sailing companions. Colin says that Gordon had a racing dinghy, a 505, which he would transport from his home on a trailer to Roa Island sailing club, and Colin would crew for him in the sea off Roa Island. They also took pupils fell-walking together, stopping at youth hostels, and Gordon would also bring along his own children. As well as the racing dinghy, Gordon was, at this time, building another boat on his drive, which he christened "The Big O". Colin helped in the construction of the boat, which was, however, not launched until summer 1977. Like others who knew him, Colin found Gordon to be totally committed to anything he did, and any project, such as boat-building, that he took on. He would never "enter anything in a half-hearted way".

Colin, in later 1976, also began to visit Gordon at home in the evenings, initially to discuss preparations for the school Christmas show, but then fairly regularly for drinks at *Bluestones*, as, because of the children, Gordon found it difficult to go out very often. Colin was aware that Carol had gone but he says that he doesn't recall ever discussing her with Gordon. During the last three months of 1976, he also observed that Gordon was in low spirits as he was constantly being "pestered" by the police, and he was actually at *Bluestones* on one occasion in December when CID officers called at the bungalow and spoke to Gordon. Colin, in a letter to his girlfriend, wrote that in January 1977 Gordon confessed to him that he was worried about "cracking up" and that he did not "feel in control".

Colin felt, during the early part of their friendship, that Gordon was "lacking in confidence", but that this changed as time went on, and especially after he joined the Gingerbread group.

Gordon Park himself, in this period following 4 September 1976, was "managing" the home and the children but "with difficulty", he later told his police interviewers in 1997. Ho took no time off work, however. He asserts that he did make attempts to find Carol, visiting the Salvation Army, and, at the suggestion of the police, putting an advert in the Barrow Evening Mail at Christmas 1976. He claims he also wrote to David Brearley, although the latter denies this. When asked about the status of his and Carol's bank accounts, Gordon was uncertain as to whether they still had a joint account in July 1976, although he says they did have one in earlier years. Either way he made no attempt to take any action to prevent Carol drawing on any joint account after her disappearance. The reality is, of course, that he would not need to take any such action.

★ ★ ★

By, say, the summer of 1979, three years after Carol had gone from his life, how was Gordon Park coping with the trauma of her 'disappearance' and having been left to manage a home and bring up three young children on his own? Yes, according to the evidence of some who knew him well, there were times when he was at a low ebb, despondent and even close to a "breakdown". But then he would have had to have been utterly devoid of emotion and sensibility if he had managed to remain at all times completely unaffected by the devastating and catastrophic way in which he had ended Carol's life, and permanently deprived three young children of their mother. He must, surely, at times have been racked by guilt and a deep sense of regret and despair. At such times he would surely have had great difficulty in concealing his state of mind from others, particularly those, like Colin Smith, to whom he was close and who were often in his presence.

At the same time, however, Gordon had clearly successfully managed to 'rebuild' his life and 'move on'. By all accounts, he was coping with the children, encouraging their interests and entertaining their friends and relations. He had carried on with his teaching career without a break and apparently with great enthusiasm. His passion for sailing and building boats had remained undimmed. He had developed new friendships and new social activities. His confidence was returning and he was 'dating' women. He never discussed his absent wife with anyone. He was, indeed, on the threshold of legally severing all his connection with her and embarking on a permanent relationship with another partner…

★ ★ ★

Catherine Sillars was a year younger than Gordon Park and the mother of five children aged, in 1978, between eight and 15 years old. She had been married to an alcoholic Glaswegian called Donald Sillars and, after he became increasingly violent towards her, divorced him in 1976. By this time, she was living in Barrow-in-Furness and working as a school meals assistant at Barrow Grammar School. It was a work colleague who introduced her to the local Gingerbread club and it was here that she first became acquainted with Gordon, who was at this time the chairman of the club.

Gordon had made no romantic overtures towards her, so it was a complete surprise to Cath when, probably in 1978, that she responded to a knock on her front door one Saturday morning, to find Gordon standing there, and his car outside with his three children in the back. Gordon's opening words were "Hi, it's little me" and he proceeded to ask Cath if she would go out "for a ride" with him. All this took place in front of Cath's children and she was heartily embarrassed by the suggestion particularly, she says, as she was not attracted to Gordon. She declined his invitation.

This was, in anybody's book, an unusual and eccentric way in which to try to kick-start a relationship with a woman who he barely knew. From what we know of Gordon Park by this time, however, it was probably not entirely out of character!

Despite this rebuff, Gordon persisted with his attempts to 'woo' Cath, and eventually, probably some weeks later, she agreed to accompany him on a car trip to the coast at Bardsea (between Barrow and Ulverston). It was a bizarre and uncomfortable occasion, with Gordon, Cath and eight children crammed into a Renault 5, and then, on arrival at Bardsea, Gordon insisting on the children moving off so he could talk to Cath alone. It was obvious to Cath that Gordon wanted to have a relationship with her, but she was averse to the idea, finding him "creepy" and his attitude disturbing. She did not however show her feelings, in case he took umbrage and abandoned her, leaving her and her children to find their own way home.

A Very Cumbrian Murder

As time went by, however, Gordon's persistence began to pay off, and, despite her reluctance and feelings of discomfort, Cath was persuaded to spend the following Christmas at *Bluestones,* together with her children, and over the next 12 months she allowed the relationship with Gordon to develop to the point where she was staying with him at his home during school holidays and on many weekends. The two families began to join in with Gordon's favourite pastimes of camping, walking, and sailing, and it was at Cath's behest that she and Gordon started to attend evening classes at Conishead Priory, near Ulverston.

Conishead Priory, otherwise known as the Manjushri Mahayana Buddhist Centre, was, and still is, a centre designed to present the mainstream of Buddhist teachings in a way that is relevant to the contemporary Western way of life, through study and meditation. As well as having a residential community, the centre also offered weekly meditation classes which could be attended by the public. It was these classes that Gordon and Cath attended between 1978 and 1981, albeit with increasing infrequency by the later date. The director of the institute at the time, Roy Tyson, found Gordon to be an intelligent man who rapidly developed an avid interest in the subject and in trying to apply Buddhist teachings in his everyday life. Roy was actually invited to Gordon and Cath's wedding in 1981, although thereafter he had no further contact with Gordon for ten years, when Gordon approached him with a view to making, and in order to make, a donation of £5000 towards the restoration of the priory. Roy's last conversation with Gordon was in January 1992 when he thanked him for the donation. Records held at the priory, however, also show that between 1983 and 1985 Gordon made annual donations to the priory, amounting in all to nearly £250. As we shall see, Cath, quite independently of her husband, did have contact with Roy Tyson during 1984 to 1985.

Cath says that Gordon took the evening classes very seriously and would spend hours at home in "meditation", often sitting alone in the greenhouse, and on one family holiday in Wales she recalls that he seldom spoke but spent almost the entire time in the garden, lost in meditation.

When interviewed by the police in 1997, Gordon explained his deep interest in Buddhism and meditation as feeling a "need to look for the truth". He agreed that he had made donations to the priory in the sums mentioned, that it was a good cause and that he had always been a contributor to charities. The interviewers strongly suggested to him that the whole Conishead phase, the meditation and the donations really sprung from a sense of guilt and a need to salve his conscience after murdering Carol. This explanation, of course, he denied, but it is one that, in retrospect, seems highly plausible.

Despite Cath's strong reservations about Gordon as a potential partner, their relationship endured for some two and a half years from that Christmas in 1978, and until Cath finally consented to becoming the second Mrs Park. If one believes her account one gets the clear impression that she had drifted into the affair against her better judgement and thereafter lacked the will-power to extricate herself from it. She did indeed 'endure' the relationship and put up with it, rather than being a wholehearted participant in the arrangement.

At first glance it is difficult to understand why Cath remained in a relationship with a man she variously described as arrogant, domineering, intimidating, sexually demanding and egocentric, and for whom she appeared to have no genuine affection let alone love.

What then is the explanation for Cath's 'endurance' in the relationship? Is she simply too weak-willed to put an end to it? Or is she frightened of repercussions if she does so? Or does Gordon have some Svengali-like hold over her? Perhaps the latter. Leaving aside the murder of his first wife, we know that Gordon Park was not routinely a man given to physical violence. Cath herself, however, perhaps gives the game away – she alludes to Gordon's uncanny ability to "manipulate my thinking through his psychology and as a teacher and his knowledge of Buddhism". He is quite able to keep Cath submissive and compliant by the application of manipulation and psychology. He doesn't need to resort to violence or threats of violence.

Some might say that, as a single woman with five children, Cath also needed her relationship with Gordon to provide some kind of emotional security, a rock to which to cling in an otherwise empty and lonely life. What tends to militate against this view, however, is Cath's own acknowledgment that the nature of the relationship itself breeds a sense of insecurity in her. During their pre-marital relationship, Gordon often asks her to marry him, but she repeatedly refuses. She is afraid of this ultimate commitment because, she says, there were "too many reasons that made me insecure". There were too many people that she met who put doubts into her mind about Gordon. Her children were either uncomfortable with him or even actively disliked him. And most of all there was the "Carol" situation. Her possessions and clothing were still in the bungalow. What if she were to return?

For Gordon the subject of Carol was "the great unmentionable". He rarely if ever spoke of her to the children or to other persons with whom he dealt. And he never spoke of her to Cath unless she broached the subject herself, and then only in brief and dismissive terms. One day, Cath says, she took her courage in her hands and actually asked Gordon if Carol was really missing or "had he killed her"? The reply she got was equally dismissive – "How can you ask me that question? You know who I am. I'm a school teacher." This did not answer the question for Cath, and she would always have this uncertainty at the back of her mind.

In 1981, however, Cath's resolve finally broke. In the early part of that year Gordon announced that he had instructed his solicitors to commence divorce proceedings against the absent Carol, and not long thereafter the marriage was formally ended on the grounds of Carol's desertion. The divorce made Cath feel somewhat more secure than hitherto and she finally agreed to marry Gordon. The ceremony took place at the Emmanuel Church in Abbey Road, Barrow on 17 July 1981, by a strange coincidence five years to the day after Carol had 'disappeared'…

★ ★ ★

The marriage of Gordon and Cath was clearly not one 'made in heaven'. Cath entertained doubts about the wisdom of the union right up to the day of the wedding. She embarked on their life together, however, cherishing the fond hope that time and their mutual commitment to the Buddhist teachings would help the marriage to work. It was indeed, however, a fond hope.

Even without the benefit of hindsight, the marriage was probably doomed from the outset. Had the union been a blissful one, or at least had there been a reasonable degree of compatibility between the partners, even then the living arrangements at *Bluestones* would have put enormous stresses on the marriage. Two adults and eight children had to be shoe-horned into three bedrooms, and whilst this may have initially been seen as something of an adventure for the members of the two families, the novelty very quickly wore off.

The situation was compounded by the behaviour of Gordon. Whatever slight optimism Cath had felt at the start of the marriage, she soon found that these feelings were misplaced. Within weeks of the wedding Gordon had "reverted to type". He began to display in abundance all those character traits with which she had been familiar before the marriage, and with which others who knew Gordon Park had long been familiar. She discovered that he would not countenance her making any changes to the décor in the bungalow or planting flowers in the garden. He demanded quiet in the house, and did not encourage conversation at mealtimes. He made it plain that he did not want Cath to form any kind of friendships with neighbours or others in the village. He wanted to control and manipulate her life and the entire domestic existence at *Bluestones*.

Gordon was also, she says, very insistent on having his privacy, and would disappear for hours into the garden or the garage to practice his meditation. Within six months, according to Cath, he had quite distanced himself from her and the rest of the family. For Cath there was no escape from the claustrophobia of life at *Bluestones*. She had given up her 'bolthole', the house she had shared with her children in Barrow, when she married Gordon. Carol had always had the diversions of her job and her various extra-marital affairs to get her out of the matrimonial home and away from Gordon, at least for a time; these avenues, however, were not open to Cath, mother of five children.

Of Gordon's friends, neighbours and relations who attended the wedding in 1981, many were soon able to detect that there were difficulties in the marriage, and most of them felt that Gordon was the principal cause of these.

Ivor and Maureen Price were at the wedding, but, family events such as christenings and funerals apart, saw little of Gordon after 1978 or thereabouts. The Price children were also less frequent visitors to *Bluestones* after Cath's family moved in. Ivor was aware of Gordon's subsequent divorce and remarriage but his only real contact with the family after this time was with Vanessa.

Gordon's stepmother, Hazel Park, was perhaps not Gordon's greatest admirer, but she became something of a confidante of Cath, particularly after the marriage foundered, and found Cath to be a likeable and genuine person. She felt Cath was being "entirely truthful" when she disclosed to her the details of how Gordon had behaved towards her and her children during the marriage. Hazel's husband, Gordon's father, died in 1983, and thereafter Hazel had little contact with Gordon, other than through solicitors, as she encountered legal difficulties in the aftermath of Sidney Park's death, largely, she says, caused by obstructive practices on the part of Gordon and his sister Barbara.

Gordon's friends and close neighbours, the McWilliams, also attended the wedding, and thought that initially the marriage was a happy one. They became aware, however, that within 12 months the relationship had badly deteriorated and become acrimonious. Both Des and Barbara became friendly with Cath from early acquaintanceship, and from her they learnt of Gordon's treatment of her and her children – such as removing the main electric fuse when he went to work in the morning, and turning off the water supply. It is quite plain that the McWilliams' sympathies lay very much with Cath, and their erstwhile friendship with Gordon cooled from this time.

Gordon's friends, Malcolm and Angela Short, both took to Cath, who they described as quiet, pleasant and caring. Both were struck by her close physical resemblance to Carol, although recognising that their personalities were very different. Neither, however, were surprised that the marriage failed so quickly – Malcom cites the immense pressures the family would have been under, living in such a confined space.

One would expect Gordon's siblings, Sydney and Barbara, to be fairly partisan in their views of the relationship and Cath, but neither, in fact, apportion any blame to Cath for the break-up of the marriage. Barbara, in particular, makes it plain that she liked Cath, and although Sydney feels that the overcrowding in the matrimonial home was the root cause of their problems, he expresses "disappointment" with Gordon over the harsh treatment meted out to Cath at the end of the marriage, when Gordon is disconnecting the central heating and disabling the telephone in an attempt to encourage Cath to leave *Bluestones*.

Hazel Park's daughter, and thus Gordon's stepsister, Rosemary Hadwin, used to see Cath regularly during her marriage to Gordon, and found her to be "a really nice person" and a good mother. She also recounts tales of Gordon's punitive conduct towards Cath as the marriage goes rapidly downhill, and leaves little doubt about where her sympathies lie. She too however has little time for Gordon generally, particularly after her stepfather's death and her mother's severe difficulties in obtaining a satisfactory settlement of his estate.

Gordon's children, when referring to the period of the marriage, are quite loyal to and supportive of their father, without expressly laying the blame for the deterioration in the relationship on Cath. They refer to constant bickering and arguments, mainly over money matters, but they clearly see the cramped and overcrowded living conditions and unsatisfactory sleeping arrangements as the main cause of tension in the household. Vanessa, in particular, finds it very uncomfortable at home and spends more and more time out of the house, and, at the age of 16, she leaves altogether to attend Newton Rigg college near Penrith.

The Sillars children, however, are overwhelmingly critical of and hostile towards Gordon. They barely have a good word to say about him. Elizabeth, for example, who was almost 16 at the time of the wedding, paints a familiar picture of control and intolerance. She alludes to the whole family being taken out for leisure activities, but these were always walking or sailing on Gordon's boat at Roa Island. Gordon's leisure interests, in other words, rather than other more family-friendly, 'inclusive' activities. She recalls a family holiday in Wales, during which, she says, Gordon largely ignored the rest of them and spent most of the time in "meditation" in the garden. She also has a recollection of his rather sadistic methods of disciplining Jeremy and Rachel – one regular event was to set an egg-timer if he felt they were eating too slowly and to insist they completed eating before the sand ran out.

Elizabeth left to go to university in the autumn of 1983, by which time the marriage was nearing its end. At one point she found that she was unable to ring *Bluestones* to speak to her mother, because Gordon had "wired up" the telephone so that it couldn't be used. Following this she received a typed letter from Gordon, sent by recorded delivery, and signed "Mr Gordon Park". The letter informed her that she was "no longer welcome at *Bluestones*". As a result of this, when she next returned to Leece, Elizabeth had to stay with Sabrine Dixon in the village and make clandestine trips to the bungalow when she wanted to see her mother. On one such occasion Gordon came back to find her there and aggressively ordered her out of the house.

Lorna Sillars, two years younger than Elizabeth, has much the same recollections of Gordon's conduct as her sister. In particular, she complains that family leisure activities were confined to walking and sailing, when the children would much rather have gone to a funfair. There was not even a one-off trip to Blackpool!

Lorna is especially vehement about events in late 1983 and early 1984. By this time, she and her younger sister Lindsay are the only two of Cath's children in full-time occupation of the home. According to Lorna, Gordon is by now clearly on a mission to drive Cath and her family out of *Bluestones*. She describes him tampering with the telephone to make it unusable; removing the fuse from the cooker whilst he was at work; and turning off the electricity and leaving them without hot water. Cath and her children, she says, had to resort to living in the middle bedroom, cooking on a small calor gas stove. Ultimately she was escorted from the premises by Gordon one day, to find her mother already outside, and the door was then locked behind them. Lorna stayed with a friend for a few days until her mother found some temporary accommodation at Conishead Priory.

The eldest of Cath's children, Donald, spent less time than the others at home. He was at college from the autumn of 1981, and, although, he dropped out after six months, he then tended to live with a girlfriend rather than at *Bluestones*. Nevertheless, he was there enough of the time to be aware of what was happening. He admits that he was prepared not to like Gordon before he met him, but then found that he disliked him more than he expected. He didn't trust him, and regarded him as a "cold fish". There were house rules, he recalls, set by Gordon. There were rooms one was not allowed to enter, mealtimes had to be strictly observed, meals were often timed with an egg-timer and Gordon insisted on "quiet" around the house. It was plain to Donald that Gordon had little or no time for him, and, once his college days were over, he was subjected to continued pressure to find employment and other accommodation. It seemed to Donald that Gordon "ruled the house". He was not physically violent to Cath, but Donald witnessed bitter arguments between them, and after one particularly ferocious exchange, he felt obliged to take hold of Gordon when he felt his mother was being threatened with violence. Gordon, however, he says, did not resist and immediately composed himself. After this incident Donald left *Bluestones* for good.

A Very Cumbrian Murder

Cath, meanwhile, was experiencing the gradual deterioration of her relationship with Gordon. She says that after 18 months of marriage, Gordon produced some "papers for a divorce" from his solicitors. He told Cath that he "couldn't live like this", although he didn't elaborate on this remark. However, after a few weeks' solitary "meditation", Gordon suddenly announced that "it would be alright" and they could "work through it". The truce did not last however, and a few months later Gordon was again talking about divorce and announced that Cath wasn't meeting his "standards or expectations". Again, however, he seemed to relent after a few days, and once again made it plain that he felt "the marriage could work".

Money was always a problem and a bone of contention, and at one point Gordon persuaded Cath to join him in a short-lived painting and decorating business. Cath found this extremely onerous, bearing in mind that she was expected as well to cook, clean and look after a number of children.

It's fair to say that the marriage was not entirely a vale of tears. There was one family holiday in Wales, and Cath and Gordon eventually had a delayed honeymoon together, touring France and Italy on a motorcycle. The former event, however, was marred by Gordon spending most of the time in lonely "meditation"; although Cath enjoyed the foreign jaunt, she makes the point that the whole trip was organised on Gordon's terms – he decided the itinerary, and he alone.

By early 1984, the end was in sight for the marriage. Gordon once again raised the subject of divorce. He became increasingly jealous, Cath says, of her speaking to neighbours or people in the village. He told her she was "unreasonable", and that he was "emotionally exhausted" and couldn't work properly. This time there was no recantation. According to Cath, Gordon began to take steps which were clearly designed to make her leave the premises. He stopped giving her housekeeping money. Her children were not allowed to eat in the kitchen, but had to remain in their bedroom to eat. He bought a second refrigerator so that each family's food could be kept separate. When he went to work, Gordon would disable the telephone, switch off the electricity, remove plugs; he then cancelled Cath's car insurance so that she couldn't drive. In May 1984, Sabrine Dixon lent Cath a primus stove so that she could cook in the bedroom, and allowed Cath and her children to wash and bathe at her home, as they had no access to hot water at *Bluestones*. It was at about this time too that Gordon wrote letters to the eldest three Sillars children, now at college or living away, to inform them that they were not permitted to return to the house.

Although she was now living in degrading circumstances, and dependent to some extent on the charity of others, still Cath did not want to leave the matrimonial home or, even it seems, give up on her marriage. In any event, she had nowhere else to go. The end came, however, during the summer holidays of 1984. Whilst Cath was outside the front door of the bungalow, retrieving the milk from the doorstep, Gordon seized the opportunity to shut and lock the front door behind her. Cath and her family were now effectively homeless, and she was driven to seek temporary accommodation at Conishead Priory. Eventually, probably in late 1984, the marriage was formally dissolved, Cath received £5000 from Gordon in the financial settlement, and she was able to move into permanent accommodation in 1985.

A Very Cumbrian Murder

It is difficult perhaps to take a balanced view on where the blame lay for the failure of the marriage, as the available evidence, or the lack of evidence to the contrary, seems to clearly point to Gordon being the culpable party, and certainly when it comes to the conduct of the parties in the last months of their time together. Gordon himself tries to redress the balance to some extent at least when he is interviewed by the police in 1997. In his view the marriage only lasted "about six weeks". He claims, in effect, that Cath had used him as a means to obtain security and a better standard of living for her and her family, and that very quickly she was showing her "true colours". She would do as she liked, he said, cook and wash up as and when she chose, and go out as and when she chose. She regarded herself as completely independent and not as a "partner" in a marital relationship. This was not what Gordon had anticipated at all, he tells the police, and before long he was "looking at ways of getting out".

He does not, however, in any way deny Cath's claims about his conduct during the remainder of and, indeed, in the last months of the marriage. He agrees with the interviewing officers that he had "quite badly treated" his wife at this time, and that it was all designed to drive her from the house. He was not "pleased with" or "proud with" his conduct at this point, but it was a means to an end, so that he and his family could return to a normal life.

Whether or not Cath was a paragon of virtue, what emerges from the 'Sillars years' is a clear and familiar picture of the man who is Gordon Park – cold, controlling, egocentric, and manipulative. These are significant, and as it will transpire, sinister features of his character. Even those features which might pass as virtues

– the careful planning, the meticulousness – will turn out to be of equal significance, as later events will show…

★ ★ ★

The apologists for Gordon Park would point to the "survival" of Cath Sillars as a clear indicator that he was no assassin, and indeed they would find further comfort in the durability of his final relationship and marriage. There is no evidence, however, that Gordon Park was a potential serial killer. The murder of Carol Park has really to be seen as a 'one-off' event, a moment in time, something that happened for its very own reasons, whatever they might have been. Apart from anything else, however acrimonious the relationship of Cath and Gordon might have become, an intelligent man such as Gordon Park would have realised that the circumstances were hardly conducive to a second wife murder. To have one wife 'disappear' might be believable; to 'lose' a second wife in a similar fashion would be too much of a coincidence and, surely, he would never get away with it. Cath, moreover, was no philanderer like Carol and no-one was going to accept that she had deserted her five children and disappeared into the wide blue yonder with a 'lover'. The children in question were, of course, of an age and of a level of awareness, that they were unlikely to have bought into such a scenario. It may have been perfectly possible to have pulled the wool over the eyes of three very young children in 1976, but the situation with Cath's children, and indeed Gordon's, was very different in the mid-1980s.

Then, too, Gordon's third wife, Jennifer, was a very different character from Carol. On the face of it, she appears to have been a loyal and understanding partner to Gordon from the start, and very much, a kindred spirit.

A Very Cumbrian Murder

There was clearly an equilibrium and a level of mutual contentment that was never or rarely reached in Gordon's earlier marriages. Disposing of his spouse would therefore have never been on his agenda.

Jennifer Park, as she became, had first met Gordon when they were both teenagers, and pupils at the Barrow Girls Grammar School and Boys Grammar School respectively. They had a "relationship", almost certainly a purely platonic one, until Jennifer discovered that Gordon had been "cheating on her" and she terminated their close friendship. From that point their paths rarely crossed for almost 25 years, during which time Jennifer left the area whilst training to be a teacher at Charlotte Mason college and then returning to Barrow to work and to marry, in 1967, another boyfriend from schooldays, Michael Marshall. Mike was to become a solicitor in Barrow, and by a strange coincidence, one of the very few times that Jennifer was to come across Gordon in this period was when she and Mike were out one night in a pub on Walney Island, and encountered Gordon in the company of Judith Walmsley. This was at the time that Gordon was engaged in the battle with Carol for custody of the children, and he took the opportunity to seek advice from Jennifer's husband on the subject.

Malcom Short was a mutual friend of both Mike Marshall and Gordon, and it was through Malcolm that Jennifer eventually learnt of Carol's disappearance, but otherwise she saw little of or heard little of Gordon until fate was to bring them together once again in 1982.

In September of that year Jennifer began teaching at South Newbarns Junior School. Gordon of course was already a teacher at the school and she was pleased to see a friendly face in the staffroom on her first morning.

Although the pair worked closely together, playing the guitar in school assemblies and producing school plays together, it wasn't until late 1986 or early 1987 that their relationship developed into anything more than just a professional one. According to Jennifer, the catalysts for this development were, firstly, the death of her father in March 1986, and then the subsequent deterioration in her relationship with her husband. Jennifer discovered that Gordon was an attentive and willing listener and a source of helpful and sensible advice at a time when she was experiencing quite severe emotional problems. Jennifer found that she was able to freely discuss her state of mind and marital difficulties with Gordon, and they could make 'common cause' as Gordon, of course, by this time had just emerged from his own period of marital strife.

Jennifer says it was in late 1986 or early 1987 that she and Gordon became "lovers". David Fisher, who married Vanessa Park in 1984, suggests that Gordon and Jennifer were emotionally involved well before this time and, indeed, whilst Cath was still living at *Bluestones*, and that Jennifer would crouch down in the front of Gordon's car when he brought her home, in an obvious attempt to avoid detection. No-one else mentions any such subterfuge, however, and it seems far more likely that the pair did not become 'an item' until after Cath had left the scene.

Despite her now firm relationship with Gordon, Jennifer remained in her marriage until late 1989. Her mother died in July 1989, leaving her the wherewithal to put down a deposit on her own home, and she left Mike shortly afterwards, following a final and bitter showdown with him. This was not, however, the end of her marriage and Jennifer seems to have continued to try to revive her relationship with Mike, even though she was openly involved in a parallel relationship with Gordon. This carried on for about two-and-a-half years, during which time she and Mike went on holiday together and spent occasional weekends together. It wasn't until 1992 that they recognised their marriage was over and they were divorced later that same year.

After leaving the matrimonial home in 1989, Jennifer was offered the temporary sanctuary of *Bluestones* by Gordon, something she regarded as "typical" of his kindness and consideration. This 'consideration' apparently extended to Gordon moving out and living with his mother during this period. Given the nature of their relationship this seems to have been an unnecessary move by Gordon, unless the pair of them were genuinely trying to give the Marshall marriage a chance to recover. If so, it seems to have been nothing more than a sham, because Jennifer acknowledges that she and Gordon were involved in a full sexual and emotionally supportive relationship throughout at least the last three years of her marriage, and she gives the clear impression that she had no intention of returning to the marriage she had already physically abandoned.

Any pretence that her marriage might still be a 'live issue' was realistically dropped when Gordon moved into 34 Norland Avenue in the Hawcoat area of Barrow on 30 November 1991. This was the home that Jennifer had bought and had moved into when she moved out of *Bluestones* in late 1989. Gordon had already decided by then to sever his ties with the house he had built so many years before, and after being on the market for about 18 months, the sale of *Bluestones* was completed in December 1991. The purchaser, one Harry Furzeland, if he didn't know about Carol Park's disappearance when he moved in, was certainly made aware of it by some of the villagers, who warned him not to do any digging in the garden because he might "find the body...". Their black humour doesn't seem to have deterred Mr Furzeland from staying in the bungalow, although he might have become less comfortable with his decision to buy it when events unfolded a few years later.

By the time of the sale of *Bluestones*, all the Park children had 'flown the nest'. Jeremy was at York university and was the father of a young son; Rachel was married and living and working in Switzerland. By virtue of their locations and careers, neither of them regularly saw Gordon after 1991, but both would visit and occasionally stay at Norland Avenue with their father and his new partner. Vanessa was married at the age of 16 to David Fisher, but by 1991 was divorced and the mother of two children. She lived in Barrow and she and her husband had had regular contact with Gordon prior to their divorce, but after Gordon's move from Bluestones, she probably saw less of him than her brother and sister, despite living in the same town.

From the time that Gordon became involved in a relationship with Jennifer, we can see a more attractive and sympathetic character emerging. Those that were close to him or worked with him in this period find him to be a much warmer and engaging personality than many of those who had known him during the time that he was married to Carol and then Cath.

David Fisher, Vanessa's sometime husband, is a notable example of this. His relationship with Gordon was initially quite cool, especially at the time of and immediately after David's marriage to Vanessa. According to David, however, as time went on Gordon became very friendly towards him and genuinely appreciative of his industry and the hard work he was putting into a marriage that had been contracted in inauspicious circumstances. David would see Gordon most weekends, as a regular sailing companion, sometimes alone, and sometimes with Vanessa and their son Andrew. He clearly held Gordon in high esteem, both as a skilful and enthusiastic sailor, and as a strong supporter of his relationship with Vanessa. Even when he and Vanessa separated, and then divorced in 1991, David says there was never any bad feeling on the part of Gordon, and Gordon continued to greet him warmly whenever they met in the street.

Neither of Jennifer's children have a harsh word to utter about Gordon, and Stuart Marshall in particular is nothing but complimentary about the man who is to become his stepfather. Not long after his sixteenth birthday, Stuart moves into 34 Norland Avenue to live with his mother, and raises no objection when Gordon moves in shortly after. Stuart describes the atmosphere as "very pleasant" and he and Gordon become "good friends". He finds Gordon to be easy-going and supportive and never ill-tempered. Stuart gets on well with all of Gordon's children, on the occasions when they visit, and when he goes away to university in the autumn of 1994, he continues to enjoy Gordon's company when he comes home between terms. He describes the situation as being like "we gained family". There is never discord and never any references to or discussion of Gordon's previous marriages.

Jennifer's daughter, Jane, was almost 18 when Gordon moved into Norland Avenue. Like Stuart, Jane was already living with her mother prior to this. Jane expresses similar sentiments about Gordon. He never tried to be a father, she says, but was always there as a "friend" and to help with odd jobs such as repairing her car. Like Stuart, she never recalls him being bad-tempered and he never raised his voice to her.

Like others before her, Jane finds Gordon to be meticulous and conscientious in every task he undertakes, and this is something that continues to be echoed by Gordon's teaching colleagues at this time. Two of his senior colleagues at Newbarns School both underline his conscientiousness as a teacher and as one who sets and maintains very high standards in his work. Both refer to one incident in 1990 when Gordon receives an oral warning following disciplinary proceedings after he has smacked two children on the bottom when they had indulged in unacceptable behaviour in the television room. It is plain that neither of the two members of staff regard Gordon's conduct as particularly serious or as evidence of a propensity to violence. It is seen by them as a sign of the times – traditional teaching methods and punishments no longer being appropriate in an age when children simply can no longer be chastised in this way. It is interesting that Jill Ward, deputy head at the school at this time, talking of Gordon in 1996, refers to him as a "valuable member of staff" who will "go out of his way to help people if he can"; further, she says, over the years he has "mellowed", "I have seen a different person in him" and "he is very happy with his current wife".

There is no doubt, however, as to who is Gordon's most ardent admirer by this time. After living together for two years, Gordon and Jennifer are married on 25 October 1993, the wedding being attended by at least some persons who have been present at Gordon's two earlier marriage ceremonies.

Jennifer describes the six years between 1991 and 1997 as "the happiest and most contented years of my life". Gordon "is a wonderful man". He is "not at all possessive" and we "rarely argue". He doesn't raise his voice and he is "never violent towards me". Jennifer's friends comment to her about the change in her personality since she had been with Gordon. "I am totally contented". Neither discuss their previous marriages.

Can this be the same Gordon Park that we have come to know, if not to love, from the years of his two ill-fated marital relationships? The meticulousness is still there, but this is a man who is even-tempered, not jealous of or possessive of his partner. A man who seems to be at peace with himself and at peace with the world, and a man who brings joy and contentment to others. A man indeed who no longer appears to be racked with guilt and haunted by his past.

What has happened? Has he indeed "mellowed"? More likely it is that he has met his soul-mate, someone who understands him and who does not confront or challenge him. Someone who, without ever knowing the facts, can help him bury the guilty secrets of his past and lead him into a bright and optimistic future.

Jennifer, of course, does not bring to their relationship the "baggage" that Cath Sillars brought; nor does she ever show the philandering tendencies of Carol Park. She and Gordon are not just teaching colleagues, but share the same interests at school of playing the guitar and producing school plays. Jennifer, unlike her predecessors, is an enthusiastic participant in Gordon's overwhelming obsession with sailing. They both have a strong interest in cycling and share a tandem. They seem to enjoy and rejoice in each other's company. They are indeed "kindred spirits". They were meant for each other. Their marriage is for sure one "made in heaven".

The fickle finger of fate, however, will not allow them to enjoy their happiness for long. Before they had been married four years, a chance discovery will rend their marital bliss asunder…

Chapter Seven

Carol: Coniston Water Gives Up a Dark Secret (August 1997)

Coniston Water is the third largest lake in the English Lake District. It is five miles long, half a mile wide and has a maximum depth of 184 feet. It has connections with art and literary figures from the recent past, in particular John Ruskin and Arthur Ransome. Ruskin, the eminent Victorian artist, art critic and philosopher, lived at Brantwood House on the eastern shore of the lake for 28 years until his death in 1900. Ransome set his children's novel *Swallows and Amazons* and its sequels around a fictional lake derived from a combination of Coniston Water and Windermere, and some of the islands featured in the books can be identified as islands in Coniston Water, such as Peel Island.

During the 20th century, Coniston Water was also the scene of many attempts to break the world water speed record by Sir Malcolm Campbell and his son Donald. The latter perished in his last such attempt on 4 January 1967, when he lost control of his hydroplane *Bluebird K7*, which then somersaulted and crashed. The remains of *Bluebird* were not recovered until 2001 and Campbell's body later the same year.

Just after 12.50 pm on Sunday 10 August 1997, a group of amateur divers from the Kendal and Lakes Sub Aqua Club launched a dive into Coniston Water from a beach adjacent to the car park at Bailiff Wood. The eastern shore of the lake is thickly wooded along most of its length, and the area known as Bailiff Wood is about halfway down this side of Coniston Water. After about 15 minutes in the water, one of the divers, David Mason, made a discovery. He was between 200 and 250 yards out into the lake, when he came across a "filled bag" resting on the silt on the lake bottom. This was at a depth of just under 25 metres according to his diving computer, and, in fact, at the top of a slope. A few metres further out and the package would have been in much deeper water and would probably never have been discovered.

The diver poked the bag and found it to be full and hard. Intriguingly, one end of the bag was tied up with what appeared to be a draw-cord and two other nylon-type cords were tied tightly around the middle and lower part of the bag. David and his diving partners decided to return to shore at this point, but with a view to returning at a later date to recover the bag.

They did in fact return three days later, armed with equipment to enable the bag to be raised and brought to shore. They managed to bring it into the shallows, where David Mason started to cut the cords round the bag. As he did so he was aware of a piece of lead falling off the package. At this point he began to suspect that "there was something wrong". He then cut the drawstring and part of the bag itself, revealing a black plastic bin liner inside the outer bag. Making a further incision into the bin liner he was horrified to see what appeared to be flesh. At this juncture it was decided that the police needed to be alerted.

Just before 9.30 pm on 13 August, Police Sergeant Griffiths and PC Baldwin arrived at the scene and were directed by some of the diving party to a location on the lakeshore about 100 yards south of Bailiff Wood car park. They walked down the banking to where the recovered package lay in the shallow water at the edge of the lake. PC Baldwin noted that the package was about four feet long and 18 inches wide. The outer packaging consisted of a canvas type bag holdall with a drawstring, not dissimilar to a kitbag. Attached to the bag with blue twine was a piece of bent lead piping. PC Baldwin proceeded to cut the outer bag with a pair of scissors, revealing a green bag underneath, and beneath this layer two dustbin-type bin liners. The officer, having cut the entire outer packaging, could then see that the innermost content of the package was a body in a badly decomposed state. The body was tied up with rope and was in the foetal position. The head was detached from the rest of the body and was loose. The body appeared to be that of a female as it was seen that a white/blue patterned nightdress remained on the torso. Sergeant Griffiths noted that the rope round the body was about half-an-inch thick and wrapped round the body at least three times and secured with knots.

Not wishing to disturb the contents of the package further the officers then secured the scene and left. In the small hours of the following morning, the body was removed to the mortuary at Furness General Hospital to await post mortem.

★ ★ ★

As soon as news broke of the discovery of a body in Coniston Water, and before there was any formal identification, there was much speculation in the press and by others that this was Carol Park. Kay Gardner, the daughter of Ivor Price, was quickly convinced the body was that of her aunt. Malcolm and Angela Short, friends of Gordon, were equally convinced, and sufficiently enough for Malcolm to ring the police to communicate his suspicions. So too did ex-Detective Constable Colin Towers.

Any doubts as to the identity of the body were quickly dispelled. The Missing Persons Bureau at New Scotland Yard had identified some 46 possibilities as to the identity and sent details of these persons to Cumbria police. Amongst the 46 cases was that of Carol, and the papers sent to Cumbria included her dental chart which had been submitted with the Missing Persons form in 1976. It was but a short step to compare Carol's dental records with the teeth extracted from the recovered body and then to formally confirm that the body was indeed that of Carol Park.

Post-mortems were conducted on 14 and 29 August 1997 by a Home Office pathologist, Dr Edmund Tapp, and a further one on 29 August together with Dr Lawler, a pathologist instructed by the solicitors for Gordon Park (who by then had been charged with Carol's murder).

The PM findings were as follows:

1) The weight which had been separated from the body by PC Baldwin consisted of flattened lead piping which had been folded over several times. Looped through a fold in the pipe was blue plastic rope.

2) The outer wrapping of the body consisted of canvas-like material which had been tied by straps at one end, and drawn together by string at the other to form a bag. This 'bag' had since been identified as a pinafore dress. Inside the bag were two small bones from the hands, two pieces of wood and two pieces of hollow metal tubing.

3) At the head end of the body, the next layer consisted of a black plastic bag which covered the head and the upper third of the body. Within this covering were skelatised remains and also a piece of strapping and two pieces of elastic material.

4) The lower part of the body was contained within green nylon material which had string running through holes along one border – it appeared to be the remains of a rucksack. There was also another black plastic bag over the lower part of the body.

5) Removal of the black plastic bag coverings showed that a length of blue nylon rope passed round the central part of the body.

6) The legs were flexed at the hips and at the knees and held in place by a thick rope which passed over the front of the shins, behind the calves and around the back. The rope was tied in a knot on the right side in the region of the hip. A length of rope also passed behind the calves and extended upwards and to the left, ending in a knot on the front of the chest.

7) A piece of rope was also looped around the left forearm and then passed three times around the upper arm before becoming continuous with loose ropes which ended in a knot.

8) A piece of thick string which had a toggle on its length was looped round the lower part of both shins. This string also passed round the lower part of the trunk and then extended between the thighs, where it was tied to a further piece of rope which passed round the middle of the trunk.

9) There were several loops of rope lying free in the region of the neck in a position which were consistent with having been round the neck of the deceased.

10) A further piece of string containing several knots was looped round the lower jaw bone which had become separated from the rest of the skull.

11) The deceased was wearing a nightdress.

12) On the inner aspect of the skull there was a prominent brown discolouration. This suggested that bleeding had occurred in this area during life.

13) The facial bones were fractured into several fragments.

14) A reconstruction of the facial bones demonstrated damage to the roots of the upper teeth. It also appeared that that the anterior border of the zygoma on the left side had a sharp edge suggesting that it had been cut rather than fractured at this site.

15) There was a fresh fracture in the 5th metacarpal bone of the left hand. The hamate bone of the left wrist was also fractured.

CAUSE OF DEATH, according to Dr Tapp, was FACIAL INJURIES and BLOWS WITH A HEAVY SHARP OBJECT.

Dr Tapp's other comments:

1) The condition of the remains was consistent with the deceased having died shortly after having been reported missing in 1976.

2) Much of the body had been preserved as a result of the cold and damp of her resting place.

3) The position in which the body had been tied up would require the body to have been extremely flexible when this was carried out. It would appear therefore that the body was tied up in this position very shortly after death and indeed during the two to four hours which would normally elapse prior to rigor mortis setting in. In Dr Tapp's opinion, it was unlikely that the body was tied up after rigor mortis had passed off – this would be three to four days after death and by that time putrefaction would have been well-established and the degree of "adipociferous change" found in the body would not have been expected (the formation of a layer of fatty tissues).

4) Extensive shattering of the upper jaw was present. This is the result of several deliberate impacts on the central part of the face. These could be in the form of blows with a heavy blunt object but more likely that the implement had a sharp edge on it, and that the central part of the face was destroyed by at least two blows in a downward direction. The destruction of facial bones, together with bleeding from such injuries, is the most likely cause of death.

5) The position of the injuries to the hands is totally consistent with them being sustained during a defensive act, such as the deceased putting her hands up to ward off blows.

Even before the post mortem, it was apparent to the police that what was required was a murder investigation. The post mortem findings only served to confirm that this was the case and that the manner in which the body had been disposed of pointed very clearly to the acts of a person who had good reason to want his or her victim not to be discovered and was prepared to go to great lengths to ensure that this was the case. The actions of a determined, diligent and meticulous individual. There was one man who ticked all these boxes. The same man who had the facility to dispose of the body two hundred yards out into a lake, inevitably involving the use of a boat. The same man who would have had some kind of motive to kill Carol Park, and the opportunity to do so. Even at the early stage of the investigation it seems unlikely that there was ever more than one suspect – Gordon Park.

In August 1997, I was the Branch Crown Prosecutor for the Cumbria branch of the northern area of the Crown Prosecution Service, and, as such, responsible for the portfolio of criminal casework in the county. At this time the police had no legal obligation to seek advice from the Crown Prosecution Service when contemplating criminal proceedings against any individual, let alone seek the consent of the service to prefer any criminal charge, no matter what the seriousness of the alleged offence. In Cumbria at least, however, it was their invariable practice to keep the CPS 'in the loop' at an early stage in investigations into such serious matters, and to listen to any advice that might be proffered. So it was, that on 22 August 1997 I met with the senior officers investigating the murder of Carol Park – Detective Superintendent Ian Douglas and Detective Chief Inspector "Ned" Kelly (the latter having been involved in an earlier murder investigation when a body was recovered from Crummock Water in West Cumbria). I was presented with an overview of the evidence, but was left with no doubt that the officers believed that Gordon Park was the killer and that they intended to arrest him and charge him with his wife's murder. I did not demur. It seemed to me that, given all the circumstances, their belief and their instinct was entirely correct and that the available evidence pointed overwhelmingly to Park as being the perpetrator…

* * *

On 10 August 1997 and in the days immediately following the recovery of Carol's body, Gordon and Jennifer Park were on holiday in France. They had travelled there on 23 July and had spent almost the entire period of their stay in a gite in Gascony. On 14 August they were joined at the gite by Gordon's friends Paul and Ann Shaw and Ann's mother. The Shaws then left the Parks on Sunday 17 August to travel on to Carcassone, and on this same Sunday morning Paul received news from his daughter in Barrow that the family dog had died. The Shaws made a decision to break their holiday and return immediately to England, and they arrived back in Barrow on the afternoon of Tuesday 19 August. Up to this point they knew nothing of the discovery in Coniston Water, but the local Barrow newspaper that night carried the story of the event and also speculation that the body might be that of Carol Park. Paul rang Vanessa Park the following day, and was told that she was aware of the discovery, and that both she and her brother Jeremy had spoken to their father in France.

Vanessa had in fact become aware during the previous weekend of the discovery, but initially had thought no more about it, believing that the death was of recent origin. It was only when it became apparent that the body may have been in the lake for as long as 25 years that it dawned on her that it might have been her mother that had been found. The police confirmed her suspicions shortly afterwards and, deeply upset, she then contacted Jeremy.

Jeremy too was aware by this time that a body had been found in the lake but, like his sister, had initially thought nothing of it. After Vanessa's call on 18 August, Jeremy decided he had to try to contact his father. It wasn't until very late the following day that he was in possession of a contact number and it was almost midnight on 19 August when he finally managed to speak to Gordon.

Jeremy told Gordon that he had some "bad news", that the police had found a body in Coniston Water, and that they believed it to be "our mum". He went on to tell his father that the CID had spoken to Vanessa and that they wanted to speak to him, Gordon, on his return to the UK. According to Jeremy, Gordon's immediate response was to utter the words "Oh dear, oh dear" and sounded shocked, hurt and suddenly very tired (on first speaking to Jeremy he had sounded "jolly", having just returned, he said, from an evening out with friends). Jeremy was concerned and worried and tried to elicit from his father if he had "done anything" or if he knew anything he ought to share with him. Gordon simply replied that he would "talk" to him, but that he would return to Cumbria. Jennifer then came on the line, but the thrust of Jeremy's conversation with her was about her daughter Jane who had been admitted to hospital with an ovarian cyst. He did, however, tell Jennifer that she needed to talk to Gordon. He then ended the call.

Jennifer, at this stage, believed that what Gordon wanted to "talk" to her about was in connection with Jane, and that Jeremy had not wanted to tell her himself. When she went to find Gordon, however, she found him sitting at the kitchen table "looking both shocked and stunned". Gordon told her what Jeremy had said about the body that

A Very Cumbrian Murder

had been recovered and that the police thought that it might be Carol. Despite the shocking nature of this news, Jennifer did not discuss the matter further with Gordon at this stage, as she was pre-occupied with the other news about Jane.

Over the next day or two Gordon spoke on the telephone to a number of people in the UK, including Vanessa, Jeremy, Forresters solicitors, Paul Shaw and, amongst others, the wife of his friend Alan Shaw. Susan Shaw had a call from Gordon on the morning of 20 August, and she disclosed that she knew about the body in Coniston Water and that there was press speculation that it was Carol. She says that Gordon was concerned about Vanessa and she agreed to try to contact her. Susan makes the point that Gordon sounded "very relaxed and basically his normal self" and that the only concerns he expressed were for Vanessa.

One would have thought that, having been made aware that his long-lost first wife may have been found dead, Gordon would have taken steps to get back to Cumbria at the first opportunity. According to Jennifer, however, they decided to stick to their original holiday plans, leaving the gite on 21 August, stopping in a guest house that night, and another in St Malo on the night of the 22nd, arriving back with the ferry in Portsmouth on 23 August. They actually got back to Barrow in the small hours of 24 August, more than four days after Gordon was first made aware of the discovery of the body. The leisurely nature of their journey home is in stark contrast to the same journey made by the Shaws on learning of the death of the family dog.

Gordon, when later interviewed by the police, was closely questioned about his reaction to being given the news of the discovery of Carol's body. His reaction, he said, was shock, and shock on two counts: firstly, because he realised that Carol had been murdered (although no-one in authority in fact had at this stage confirmed that this was the cause of death, and not accident or suicide); and secondly because he knew that the police would link the death to him, given that the police interviewers in 1976 had told him that he was the "prime suspect" if Carol were to be found dead.

It was put to him by the interviewing officers that his conduct following receipt of the news was strange and not normal. In the first place, why had he not contacted the police in Barrow? He had, after all, rung a number of other people, but not the one set of people who could have really told him what was going on, and what were the precise circumstances of his first wife's death. Surely he would have wanted much more information than his family or friends could give him. Gordon's response to this was that he had thought of contacting the police but had decided to leave it until he "got home". Then, why hadn't he set off immediately on the homeward journey? Well, said Gordon, it didn't seem possible to get home earlier – the accommodation for the following days was booked and so was the return ferry journey.

The reality of course is that he didn't need to ring the police to find out what had happened. He knew perfectly well how Carol had met her end. He couldn't of course have known how matters were going to turn out for him in early 1998, but at this point he didn't know the nature and quality of the evidence against him and he must have believed that 'the game was up', and that on his return to Barrow he would be arrested, charged, tried and imprisoned. He would have no incentive at all to expedite the process, to rush back to England and to curtail what would probably be his last few days of freedom…

Chapter Eight

Gordon: Arrest, Investigation, Charge and Discontinuance
(August 1997 to January 1998)

At 8.20 on the morning of Sunday 24 August 1997, police officers attended 34 Norland Avenue, Barrow-in-Furness, where Gordon Park was arrested on suspicion of having murdered Carol Ann Park on or about 17 July 1976.

The premises had already been searched on 22 August, before the Parks had returned to England, under the authority of a search warrant. A number of items had been seized, including hammers, a ring, ropes and string. The same day, lengths of rope were also retrieved from a yacht, *Mrs J*, belonging to Park and moored on Coniston Water.

On 20 August officers had also carried out a search of *Bluestones*. The bungalow was now occupied by Harry Furzeland, who had purchased the property from Gordon Park in December 1991. Mr Furzeland had been able to point out to the police various items that had been left on the property by the vendors and which were seized by the officers. These items included a toilet bowl from the garage, scrap lead piping from the garage and a quantity of ropes from the garage and the loft.

From the time the body was recovered, and as soon as it became clear that there had been 'foul play', Cumbria police had launched a full-scale murder investigation: a completely different affair from the relatively low-key 'missing person' enquiry of 1976. Statements were taken from relatives, friends, neighbours and work colleagues of the Parks, including known former lovers of the deceased and also the Sillars family. Enquiries were pursued with persons with experience in forensic casework who could give expert opinions on such evidential material as the lead piping recovered from the body and elsewhere, and the knots and ropes found from the same sources. Enquiries were made into Gordon Park's sailing history, the boats he had owned and any connection he may have had with Coniston Water. There were enquiries also into the whereabouts in July 1976 of John Paul Rapson, the convicted murderer of Carol Park's sister Christine.

From the outset, the investigation was hampered by two significant factors. In the first place, the trail was cold. The offence, and there was no doubt that there had been an offence, had almost certainly been committed more than 20 years ago. Potential material witnesses in many instances were infirm or dead, or simply had only a poor recollection of occurrences in 1976 and before that time. Some of the police officers involved in the 1976 enquiry were again either dead or unable, or even unwilling, to assist their 1997 counterparts. There was unlikely to have been by this time any incriminating evidence to be found at the scene of the likely murder – ie. *Bluestones,* or indeed in any boats or vehicles owned by Gordon Park, or on any potential murder weapon. Any clothing that might have borne evidence of the killing was long gone.

Then there was the missing file of the 1976 investigation. The 1997 investigators were working in a vacuum. They had no real idea of which witnesses had been interviewed in 1976, or what those witnesses might have said to the officers then, and whether what they were saying now was consistent with their earlier statements. They had no idea of what views the senior investigating officers then had of the results of the enquiry – there was no record and the officers were dead. They had no idea of the circumstances in which Park was interviewed in 1976 or of the content of those interviews – a situation that Park was able to exploit again and again to his advantage.

Despite the difficulties facing the 1997 investigators, they had two 'positives' with which to work: an immutable body of circumstantial evidence that pointed strongly to Park's guilt, and an unshakeable conviction that they had 'got the right man'.

★ ★ ★

The content of many of the witness statements referred to above has been alluded to previously in this narrative. There are, however, other witnesses whose stories or evidence now become important in the context of the murder investigation.

One category of witness that comes under particular scrutiny at this time is that of Carol's former lovers; another such witness is John Paul Rapson. These of course are persons who might be regarded as having a possible motive for murder.

Of the ex-lovers, Colin Foster, had moved to Scotland with his family in 1975. There is no evidence that he was back in the Furness area in July 1976, nor that he has had any contact with Carol since some time in 1974, nor that he would have the means or the necessary skills to dispose of Carol's body in the manner or location in which it was found. It is also highly improbable that he would have had any motive for killing a woman with whom he has had no romantic connection for more than two years. It seems that he was never regarded as a potential suspect and he was never treated as such in the 1997 investigation.

David Brearley, of course, had been more recently involved with Carol than Colin Foster, and a police officer who interviewed him in early 1977 indicates that he had "misgivings" about Mr Brearley's account of his movements in or about July 1976. At the end of the day, however, he is no more a likely suspect then Foster and, again, it seems, was never regarded as such.

In a statement he made to the police in August 1997, Brearley refers to a conversation he had with Carol during the currency of their relationship, in which Carol tells him she "had something" over Gordon which she believed she could use in the forthcoming battle over custody of the children. According to Brearley, Carol told him that her husband and his father had been involved in tax avoidance in connection with the decorating business, and that Gordon had personally taken sums of money to deposit in a bank in the Isle of Man. The 'punchline', however, was, Carol told Brearley, that Gordon had threatened her that if she tried to use the information, she would "end up in the deepest lake". If the threat was made, it would be both highly significant and prescient. Both of Brearley's brothers, and also a friend, Irene Earl, in witness statements made to the police in 1997, indicate that Brearley told them of these threats, either at a time when he was still involved with Carol or at the time of her disappearance in 1976. His re-iteration of this information to a number of third parties may tend to support the contention that Carol had said what he claims she had said, although not necessarily that the threats had been made by Gordon in the first place. Whilst the information is very interesting, and on the face of it significant, it is of purely academic interest since it was never likely to be admissible evidence against Gordon Park in his ultimate trial. It will come as no surprise that in his 1997 interviews with the police Gordon vehemently denied that he had ever made such threats, or indeed had ever been in a position to indulge in such tax avoidance schemes.

Alan Walls, between 1975 and 1977, was a detective sergeant in Cleveland Constabulary stationed at South Bank police station in Middlesborough, and at some time in this period he was contacted by Cumbria police and asked to interview David Brearley regarding the disappearance of Carol Park. He recalls, and his official police notebook confirms, that it was not until January 1977 that he was able to carry out this task. His memory by 1997 was hazy as to the account given by Brearley, but he recalls interviewing him over three hours and being "dissatisfied" with Brearley's story as to his movements over the time that Carol disappeared. By 1997, however, he is unable to be more specific as to his 'misgivings', and any statement he made in 1977 and the statement he took from Brearley at this time have, of course, been lost.

David Brearley himself maintains that he told Walls of the "threats" mentioned by Carol and that he was convinced that her disappearance was the result of her being murdred by Gordon Park. He states that the officer asked him if he had murdered Carol, although Brearley did not believe that the question was a serious one. He says, furthermore, that he was never interviewed under caution as a suspect, and, of course, as a former police officer himself, he would have appreciated the difference between being interviewed as a witness and being treated as a suspect.

A Very Cumbrian Murder

Brearley's ex-wife Margaret Hirst told the police in 1997 that he had been violent towards her on two occasions before they parted, and she also recalled a phone conversation with him in about 1976 when Brearley told her that the woman with whom he had previously been in a relationship had "disappeared" and that the police were going to dig up his garden because they believed he had killed her. According to Ms Hirst, he told her that the police may be in touch with her and "make sure you tell them that I am a really nice bloke". She claimed that Brearley told her that his relationship with Carol was "stormy" and on one occasion she saw a scratch on his face, which he said was inflicted by Carol in a fight with him. She formed the impression that her ex-husband was "scared" by the police interest in him and that he believed that they thought he might have had something to do with her disappearance.

Despite the observations of Detective Sergeant Walls and Margaret Hirst, the notion that David Brearley might have killed Carol is entirely fanciful. In July 1976 he was teaching full-time in the Teesside area, and his brother Raymond, also a teacher in the same area, confirms that the local schools did not break up until Wednesday 21 July. David was also taking in lodgers at this time and also had his son Michael to look after. Michael was then nine years old and in his father's full-time custody. In the week that the summer term ended, David says that he had to prepare for Michael going to cub camp, and he then became involved in a local Eisteddfod, accommodating participants at his home. On 31 July he met a Slovakian dancer called Viera, who was involved in the event and staying in a local hostelry. Viera subsequently became his second wife.

Given the extent of his commitments in July 1976, the likelihood of David Brearley having travelled to Leece from the north-east, brutally murdering Carol, and elaborately and expertly trussing her up and disposing of her body seems remote indeed. The time and opportunity to cross the Pennines to do the deed was extremely limited. There is, neither, any obvious motive – his parting from Carol does not seem to have been acrimonious, and there is no evidence that he was harbouring any grudge or had made any attempt to contact her after the end of their relationship, which was some 12 months previously. Finally, there is no evidence that he had any expertise in tying knots or sailing, or any knowledge of Coniston Water or, indeed, the means to dispose of a body there. It does not appear, indeed, that he was ever regarded by Cumbria Constabulary as a suspect for the murder of his former lover.

If anything, John Paul Rapson was a more likely candidate for the role of killer. He was a convicted murderer, and, indeed, had already killed one female member of the Price family. Moreover, although sentenced to life imprisonment in 1969, from March 1976 he was frequently being granted 'home leave' at weekends. The meant he would return for the weekend to live with his mother in South Row, Barrow. Although he has no recollection of specific dates when this occurred, it seems very possible that he was in Barrow on 17 July 1976.

This, however, is the high-water mark of the case against Rapson. He had no clear motive for murdering the adoptive mother of his daughter. In his statement made to the police in 1997, he expresses no resentment about the adoption and, indeed, says that "it was the right thing to do". At the time of this statement it appears that he had never tried to contact Vanessa since she was adopted by the Parks. He maintained, and there is no evidence to the contrary, that he had never owned or even driven a car, had no interest in or ability to sail a boat, had never been a climber and had never owned any ropes or climbing equipment. Again, therefore, this is someone who had not the motive, the wherewithal or the expertise to have committed this crime. He can surely be ruled out of the reckoning, and the investigators seemed to have done so.

★ ★ ★

Another line of enquiry in 1997 was into Gordon's ability and experience as a sailor, whether he owned or had regular access to a boat in July 1976 and whether he regularly sailed on Coniston Water at that time. In interview with the police in 1997, Gordon tried to present himself as not the owner of a boat in July 1976, and as only an infrequent user of Coniston Water at that time and in the months and years immediately leading up to Carol's disappearance. Neither claim is borne out by the evidence of others. Vanessa recalls sailing on Coniston with her father and other family members prior to July 1976. Ernie Shaw says that from the 1960s to the 1990s he regularly travelled on Coniston Water with Gordon and his family, and that Gordon either had a boat or had access to his father's boats at any given time. Des McWilliams recalls the Park children telling him in the period before Carol went to live with David Brearley that they often went out with their father in boats, and that their "favourite place" was Coniston. Colin Smith was a regular sailing companion of Gordon by July 1976, including on Coniston Water, and in Gordon's 505 sailing dinghy. Colin states that Gordon also had a trailer for transporting the boat.

It is in June or July 1976, of course, that Colin and Gordon are on the sailing course at Tower Wood, a course in which Gordon was awarded an "advanced certificate", a clear illustration of his extreme competence as a sailor.

An interesting piece of evidence in connection with Gordon's association with Coniston Water comes from one Ian Stancliffe, who was secretary of Coniston Sailing Club from 1967 until 1996. He says that in 1997 he had known Gordon as a sailor on the lake for at least 20 years, and he asserts, by necessary implication if not expressly, that Gordon sailed there before Carol disappeared. At the time that Carol had left the scene, says Mr Stancliffe, Gordon stopped coming down to Coniston Water "for some considerable time". This, of course, would be quite understandable.

★ ★ ★

The 'expert' evidence sought and gathered by the investigators in 1997 centred round the lead piping which had been attached to the 'package' recovered from the lake, the nightdress on the body and the ropes and knots on the package and body. No doubt the passage of time or the watery grave would have defeated any prospect of recovering any other scientific evidence linking the body to the killer or the killing to *Bluestones*.

A forensic scientist, Philip Rydeard, examined the lead piping from the body, lead piping and the toilet bowl recovered from *Bluestones*, and hammers recovered from 34 Norland Avenue. The piping from the body consisted of a length of flattened and folded lead pipe, some 67 inches in length. Mr Rydeard felt that the length and appearance of the piping was "suggestive" of it being the cistern pipe from a high-level toilet installation. The

A Very Cumbrian Murder

piping was also seen by a local plumber who described it as a "high-level system flush pipe", the type of piping which would have been used locally in old properties before low-level toilet systems were fitted. In interview, Gordon told the police that he had replaced the toilet system after Carol had left, but he had installed the original one when he built the bungalow and this was not of the type referred to above. Mr Rydeard did, however, find that the toilet bowl recovered had an inlet spigot at the rear to accommodate the pipe from a cistern, and that it would have been a fit for piping of the diameter of the lead piping from the body. He also found that one of the hammers had a flat head which was similar in size to the indentations on the lead piping, but was now too worn to be properly assessed for that purpose. Gordon Park denied that any of the hammers had been in his possession in 1976, saying that he had "acquired" them during later years and during one or other of his subsequent marriages.

The sum total of this expert's conclusions was that there was "some evidence" to "associate" the lead pipe with the toilet bowl, but only in relation to size; and that there was "some evidence" that hammer marks on the flattened lead pipe were made by one of the hammers "when in a less worn state".

It should be apparent that this evidence was of very limited value and, taken on its own, probably of no value at all. The best that could be said of it was that taken at its highest and in conjunction with <u>all</u> the evidence against Park, it might provide some extremely modest support for the proposition that the lead piping originated from *Bluestones* and had been attached to the body by Gordon Park.

The nightdress which the deceased was wearing was identified from photographs by a director of a mail order clothing firm called Halwins, a firm which was trading in the 1970s, as a product which was briefly for sale in 1971. Bearing in mind that Carol was almost certainly murdered and her body disposed of in 1976, this evidence advances the case not at all. What is far more significant, however, is the fact that the body was 'wearing' a nightdress of any sort. This has to lead to the very reasonable assumption that Carol was killed whilst in her nightwear and in her own home. Park, in interview, claims not to "recognise" the nightdress as having belonged to Carol, but, even if he is being honest about this, it is not surprising that he has no recollection of all her nightclothes after more than 20 years, and he had good reason not to be honest about it. The notion that a third party had killed her in another place and then clothed the body in another's nightdress seems highly unlikely to say the least? Given that the evidence points very strongly to Carol being killed either late on Friday 16 July or early on 17 July 1976, it can be no surprise that she would have been in her nightwear at the time and, in these circumstances, surely in her own home.

No less compelling evidence, in my view, was that provided by Roger Ide, a highly qualified and experienced consultant forensic scientist, whose specialism consisted in giving expert opinion on knots and ligatures. He examined the ropes and cords associated with the body, and also those associated with Gordon Park.

Mr Ide found that the improvised fastening at the hem of the pinafore dress, which formed the outer covering of the body, consisted of a short length of twine which had been threaded through the hem of the dress, penetrating the material no less than 14 times, the twine then being pulled tight and tied with three successive overhand knots. The loose ends of the twine beyond the knots had been trimmed, probably with scissors, leaving two short ends protruding from the knot. The whole operation, according to Mr Ide, demonstrated "meticulous attention to detail in the circumstances".

The mouth of the rucksack, which had encased the lower part of the body, as an inner layer of the packaging, had been designed to be closed by means of a draw-cord operating through metal eyelets around the mouth. The draw-cord consisted of synthetic cord tied to a central eyelet with an overhand loop. In addition, however, "figure-of-eight" knots had been tied at each end of the cord.

A length of buff-coloured string had been tied round parts of the body, and then tied with two "half-hitches" to another part of the string. There was a tight overhand knot tied at the end of the string, probably, states Mr Ide, to stop it unravelling.

Another piece of cord found on the body had been heat-sealed with a flame at one end, and attached to the thin end of the cord with a "sheet-bend" knot. There is a piece of string which has an overhand knot near one end, apparently to stop it unravelling, and one end of the string has been threaded through the eyelet of a spring clip and made fast with an "eye splice". The end of the splicing had been heat-sealed with a flame according to Mr Ide.

Another long length of rope from the body is examined by Mr Ide and again he finds that one end has been heat-sealed. At the other end a slip knot had been tied, and further along the rope a fixed loop had been formed with a double overhand knot; further on still a double loop knot had been tied, with one fixed loop and one constricting; and further on still there was a region where two lengths of the rope had been twisted together forming a natural loop.

The lead weight which had been attached to the body incorporated a length of blue rope, which was examined by Mr Ide in conjunction with another piece of blue rope which had originally been tied to the middle of the lead weight. The first piece of rope had been heat-sealed at one end and near to both ends there had been tied a "figure-of-eight" knot. Also a strong loop had been formed by tying a "bowline" knot near to one end, and the rope had then been wrapped round a large item and then tied to the bowline with either a "reef knot" or two half-hitches. The other piece of rope had been tied to the other, either with a reef knot or two half-hitches, and its end had again been heat-sealed. There was an "eye splice" at the other end of this rope.

Most of the knots and splices referred to above were found on ropes and cords recovered by the police from *Bluestones*, 34 Norland Avenue and from *Mrs J*, a boat owned by Park at the time of his arrest. These included examples of bowline, sheet-bend, figure-of-eight, reef knot and eye splice, as well as instances of ends of ropes being heat-sealed.

The bowline, says Mr Ide, is a "well-regarded" knot normally used to form a fixed loop. Gordon Park would have learnt how to tie the knot in the scouts and it is a knot used routinely by rock-climbers, and, according to Mr Ide, also by sailors. In my experience, there would not be that many people outside the climbing and sailing fraternities who would know how to tie a bowline.

A Very Cumbrian Murder

The sheet-bend is even more of an esoteric knot. It is used as an effective method of attaching two ropes of unequal thickness to each other. Gordon would have learnt it in the scouts, as I did, but it has no obvious application in climbing or sailing. I would be extremely surprised if more than 1% of the population could tie a sheet-bend today, or, indeed, in 1976.

Figure-of-eight knots are generally used as "stopper" knots, by sailors apparently and also by climbers. I cannot remember learning this knot in the scouts, but picked it up later as a rock climber. As would Gordon Park. Hardly, therefore, a knot in common use.

The reef knot is more common, and would be quite widely used for tying up parcels, for example. As Mr Ide points out, however, most people tend to tie "granny" knots rather than reef knots. Tying a reef knot correctly may demonstrate a certain amount of familiarity and expertise.

An eye splice, according to Mr Ide, is regarded as the most effective way of forming a permanent fixed loop in a traditional three-strand rope. It is a technique used by sailors, and can be regarded as "demonstrating some skill in the manipulation of ropes". Again it is likely that Gordon would have picked up the ability to make an eye splice whilst in the scouts.

Furthermore, heat-sealing the end of ropes is not something the man in the street would be routinely carrying out. It is done to prevent the ends of ropes from fraying, by persons accustomed to handling ropes.

When interviewed in 1997, Gordon freely acknowledged an ability to tie all of the above knots and splices and to have used them in his climbing and sailing activities. Moreover, he accepted that he never threw away string and ropes and that the cordage recovered by the police from the two addresses and his boat would be his and that he would be the author of the knots in them.

Mr Ide, in his conclusions, is of the opinion that several of the knots used to secure the body "demonstrate a degree of knot tying skill consistent with the person who tied them having had an interest in sailing, climbing or some activity associated with knot tying". Gordon Park, of course, ticks all three of these boxes!

Mr Ide cannot, of course, say that the same person has tied the knots on the body and on the ropes recovered from the two houses associated with Park – that would be surely quite impossible!

What is very clear, however, is that the manner in which the body has been wrapped up and tied is extremely elaborate and is the work of someone with a significant degree of expertise in knot tying and of a very diligent and meticulous disposition. To my mind, if one once again takes this in conjunction with all the other evidence – the timing, the way in which the body is disposed of and concealed, the way in which it is dressed – together with motive, opportunity and facility, then the case against Park as the killer is utterly compelling.

* * *

Following his arrest, over the next 36 hours Park is interviewed on ten separate occasions at Barrow police station by Detective Sergeant Mike Warner and Detective Constable Doug Marshall. His solicitor, Mike Graham of Forresters solicitors, is present throughout these interviews.

The interviews cover a wide range of subjects – the history of Gordon's relationship with Carol, their family, the building of *Bluestones*, Carol's affairs with Foster and Brearley, the events of 17 July 1976 and Carol's final 'disappearance', his reporting her as missing on 4 September 1976, his passion for sailing and boats, his climbing experience, his knowledge and experience of knot tying and his second and third marriages. Most of the content of those interviews, including Park's responses to questions, and his strategy of referring the interviewers to the "statement I made in 1976", have been alluded to previously in this narrative. He continued to deny throughout the interviews that he was responsible for Carol's death.

Despite his denials of the offence for which he was being interviewed, at shortly after 8.00 pm on the 25 August, Gordon Park was charged with the murder of Carol Ann Park on or about 17 July 1976. His response to the charge was "I am innocent of this charge".

★ ★ ★

On 26 August 1997, Park appeared before Furness and District Magistrates' Court and was remanded in custody for seven days. His solicitor, Mike Graham, made no application for bail on his behalf at this time, and bail was refused on the grounds that there was a substantial likelihood that the defendant might interfere with witnesses, might fail to surrender to bail and for his own protection. I appeared for the prosecution at the hearing, and whilst it was probably desirable that Park be remanded in custody at this stage, I felt that a time would come when he could be safely released on bail, subject to appropriate conditions. He was a man of hitherto unblemished character and it seemed unlikely that he was going to commit further offences, let alone of the type with which he was charged. Cath Sillars and Jennifer Park were living examples of his lack of propensity to be a serial wife killer! Nor, it seemed to me, was he likely to abscond – all his roots and family connections were in the area, and it would scarcely be in his interests to do so. If there was any residual danger of him approaching witnesses, this could be countered by a bail condition which would remove him well away from south Cumbria. The "own protection" ground for custody arose from a fear that he might commit suicide, a fear commonplace with this type of charge, but it did not seem very likely at this time that Park was a candidate for taking his own life.

Following the court hearing, I went to the police station and witnessed a briefing to the police investigative team given by the senior investigating officer, Detective Superintendent Ian Douglas. His final words to his officers were these: "We've charged the bugger, now let's go out and get the fucking evidence." To the uninformed listener this direction might appear slightly alarming, the implication being perhaps that there was little or no evidence against Park! This, however, would be a totally false impression. To my own knowledge, there was not a single police officer involved with the case, at any stage following the recovery of the body, that did not firmly believe that the evidence was sufficient to prove Park's guilt. A view that I certainly shared. Ian's words were, and were intended to be, flippant, and amounted to no more than a request to 'dot is and cross ts' and take any outstanding witness statements. Unfortunately, the views that the police and I held about the sufficiency of the evidence proved not to be shared by my superiors in the Crown Prosecution Service…

Within a few days of Park being charged, the storm clouds were already gathering. I was summoned to a meeting in Newcastle with the senior management team of the northern area of the Crown Prosecution Service, and there I was asked to give a summary of the evidence in the case, or at least as I understood the evidence at that point. From the outset I detected a distinct lack of enthusiasm for the case.

Of the three-man team I faced, only one had any regular involvement in casework. Mike Graham, the Chief Crown Prosecutor, was an experienced and very able lawyer and I had enormous respect for his views. Of the other two, David Farmer, Mike's deputy in effect, had not been involved in casework for some time; the other person was not a lawyer at all. What was a little disturbing was that all three, including Mike, were so dismissive of the strength of the case against Park when their information about it was second-hand, and before they had seen the actual evidence. Certainly I did nothing to encourage such a view. They were, however, persuaded to reserve judgement until they had seen the file of written evidence when it became available, and to seek the views of leading counsel before any irrevocable decision about the case was taken. To me, however, it appeared that the 'writing' was probably already 'on the wall'...

On my return to Cumbria, I relayed the views of my superiors to the senior police officers. They were disappointed, if not perhaps as surprised as I expected them to be. We resolved to present the case in the best light we could in an attempt to convert the 'doubters'. Nonetheless, we agreed, in the circumstances it would be appropriate to withdraw the objections to bail, something, of course, I had in mind in any event.

On 9 September, at a further court hearing, the magistrates were told there was no objection to the defendant having bail, providing suitable conditions could be found. As a result, Park was released on bail with conditions that he lived with his sister in Manchester, observed a curfew, surrendered his passport, reported twice a week to the police station in Tyldesley, did not approach prosecution witnesses and, except in very restricted circumstances, did not return to Cumbria. These were conditions with which he successfully complied throughout the remainder of the life of the case at this time.

Some six weeks after Park was released on bail we (the CPS) received from the police the full file of the evidence they had gathered in the 1997 investigation. For all intents and purposes, this was the sum total of the evidence as nothing more of significance was found thereafter, not in 1997 anyway. This was the opportunity for us to form a 'brains trust' to consider the file – ie. the special casework lawyer Ken Hay, the local divisional Crown Prosecutor in Barrow, Phil Bates, and myself. Between us we had more than 50 years' experience of prosecuting and of evaluating the evidence in all manner of criminal cases. Though I say it myself, this was the best possible collection of minds available in Cumbria to weigh up and assess the evidence in this case.

We spent a whole day at the end of October dissecting the case, discussing it in detail, and identifying strengths and weaknesses (we had all read the evidence before we met). To cut a long story short, although we recognised there were some weaknesses in the evidence, we were all agreed that that evidence provided a realistic prospect of conviction against Park and that the case should continue to trial.

Following this 'local' review we sent the full file of evidence to the area headquarters of the Crown Prosecution Service in Newcastle for the attention of the Chief Crown Prosecutor, together with a strongly-worded exposition of our own views on the case, and indeed those of the police. I had little doubt, however, that our views would not prevail, and I was soon to be proved right in this regard.

At the end of November 1997, Mike Graham, the Chief Crown Prosecutor sent us a copy of his own critical review of the evidence, which incorporated his final opinion that there was not a realistic prospect of conviction. Whilst he identified the same weaknesses in the case as we had done earlier, he saw them rather as weaknesses that could not be answered or explained, and consequently as undermining any real prospect of a jury finding Park guilty of murder. Those identified weakness were as follows:

1. The evidence of the neighbour, Sabrine Dixon, that she had seen a blue VW Beetle on the driveway of the Parks' home on the day of the visit to Blackpool, ie. 17 July 1976.

2. There were others who may have had a motive for murder – Carol's ex-lovers, and Gordon's ex-girlfriends, and Rapson.

3. The time-frame within which Carol must have been murdered, her body trussed up before rigor mortis set in and the corpse disposed of in Coniston Water. Although not impossible, it would have presented enormous difficulties to do all this in the time

available and it would have involved leaving the children alone in the house.

4. If the killing took place at *Bluestones* how could this be achieved without alerting the children, and without leaving any trace of a struggle or of a brutal murder with a weapon?

5. The lapse of time since 1976 meant that there may have been witnesses who are no longer available, or whose memories by 1997 may be no longer reliable. It also meant there was no opportunity now to investigate or test Park's movements in 1976. The trail, in other words, had gone cold.

6. The loss of the Missing Person file, allied to the 21 year delay, meant that there was scope for the defence to argue that the prosecution was "an abuse of the process" of the court, since it may not be possible for Park to have a fair trial as what witnesses said in statements in 1976 could not be compared with what they were saying in their statements now, and, more importantly, there may have been other witnesses, now unidentifiable or unavailable, who could have provided significant information, which may of course have assisted the defendant.

All of these points, although good ones, are, to my mind, and were then, quite capable of being answered or being put in perspective:

1. The evidence of Sabrine Dixon was discussed in chapter five. Its accuracy or relevance is highly questionable and it can be easily discounted.

2. Carol's former lovers and Rapson as potential murderers were considered earlier in this chapter and

can be discounted on the grounds of lack of resources, time, opportunity and expertise, even if they had a motive, which is unlikely. Equally, any suggestion that a jealous or vengeful Judith Walmsley could have carried out such an elaborate plan is just as fanciful.

3. The probable time-frame within which the murder was committed, the body trussed up, taken to Coniston and then transported to its place of disposal may well have been short and complicated by logistical problems. The point is, however, that any other person would have been confronted with the same operational difficulties. Park at least was the man on the spot and may well of course have been carrying out a pre-conceived plan. The planning and execution of the enterprise, with all its difficulties, are typical of the man, bearing as they do all the hallmarks of care, application and meticulousness. There is also the possibility that, having secured the body, Park then placed it in temporary storage until such time as he could conveniently remove it to its final resting place. Kay Gardner remembers that there was a chest freezer in the garage.

4. If, as seems most likely, the murder took place in the house and during the evening or night of 16/17 July, the children, it seems, would also have been in the bungalow at the time. There may well have been at least some noise of a struggle and resistance, but then the children, if they were awake or awakened at the time, were not unaccustomed to the sound of their parents bickering or loudly arguing. It is quite possible, of course, that Carol was not expecting violent conduct and had no time for more than token

resistance or being able to sound the alarm before she was brutally despatched. Clearly there would have been a good deal of blood, wherever the fatal blows were delivered. If this was in the matrimonial bedroom, then Park would have had to carry out a major cleaning-up operation after disposing of the body. In this connection, it seems that the children were not allowed into the bedroom to see their mother before they were taken off to Blackpool the following morning, and then Gordon had several weeks to 'dispose of the evidence'. When the police did become involved, it was only to conduct a 'missing person' inquiry and it was quite likely, of course, that this would not include a detailed forensic examination of the house. By 1997 the chances of recovering any material evidence from such an examination had probably gone. It is not impossible, of course, that Carol had initially simply been rendered unconscious and that the act of murder had been carried out after she had been removed from the house.

5. It was always recognised that the 21 year gap and the loss of the Missing Person file could lead to a successful application by the defence at trial that the proceedings should be stopped by the judge as an "abuse of process", as the defendant could not, in these circumstances, have a fair trial. Such applications had enjoyed a measure of success in the 1980s in cases of child abuse where the allegations against the defendant were 'historic', often of offending 20 or more years previously. By 1997, however, this had become a much less fruitful area for the defence in cases of 'delay'. Courts, more and more, were taking the view that the trial process itself

provided adequate protection for defendants in such cases, the judge being able to direct the jury of the need to exercise caution when relying on evidence of alleged offending many years ago, and that the defendant may have been deprived of the opportunity of identifying or calling witnesses who may no longer be known or available. As it turned out, it was never a successful avenue for the defence in this instance, even in 2005 when the delay was even greater and there was also a delay between the charge being dropped in 1998 and being revived in 2004.

What I believe was the real reason, however, for CPS area management, and subsequently leading counsel, having no faith in the strength of the case was the fact that there was no direct evidence to tie Park to the killing or the disposal of the body. There was no DNA or other scientific evidence. There were no confessions. There was no 'smoking gun'. The case against Gordon Park relied entirely on 'circumstantial evidence' – ie. evidence that relies on <u>an inference</u> to connect it to a conclusion of fact.

This was an accurate assessment of the nature of the evidence. It was entirely circumstantial. But the point is that there is no bar on persons being found guilty of criminal offences purely from such evidence, always assuming the circumstantial evidence is strong enough and compelling enough to enable the jury to draw the appropriate inference(s). I have already previously in this book referred to the case of Shatanawi – a case where the evidence was entirely circumstantial and there wasn't even a body, but the defendant was convicted of murdering his wife. I shall refer later to another notable Cumbrian murder case, that of Robert Wilson, who was also convicted of murdering his wife on evidence which again was purely circumstantial. And these are by no means the only examples of such cases. It is noteworthy that in November 2008, three Court of Appeal judges, when rejecting Park's appeal against his conviction, stated that there was a "strong circumstantial case against the defendant".

I always believed at this time that the circumstantial case against Park was very strong, indeed utterly compelling. Furthermore, it seemed to me, that those who thought otherwise were taking the wrong approach to the evidence. They were looking for direct evidence that confirmed that Park was the killer, that he was more than the 'prime suspect' (and even the detractors of the case seemed to accept that he was this!). Because there wasn't any such evidence, then one couldn't rule out the possibility that it was someone else. This was a traditional, clinical approach. To me, however, the commonsense and proper approach was to look at the case 'through the other end of the telescope' – ie. to consider that, if it wasn't Park, who else could it possibly be? Once one had ruled out the other options, then by a process of elimination one was only left with one: Gordon Park.

This, I think, was the strategy that was ultimately adopted at Park's trial in 2005. The starting point was that it was inconceivable that this was a 'stranger killing' – there would be absolutely no reason for a "passing stranger" to wish to tie up the body in such an elaborate fashion and then dispose of it in such a way. The murder had to be committed by someone who did not want the body to be found or, indeed, the fact of murder to be discovered.

A Very Cumbrian Murder

This of course would reduce the number of suspects to a handful – indeed, to the few persons who would realise that suspicion would fall on them if the body was found. We have already considered the possibility that Rapson, Foster, Brearley or Walmsley might be responsible for Carol's murder and discounted it. They all lacked the resources, facility, expertise or opportunity to carry out the murder and its aftermath. Nor do any of them have any obvious motive for murder.

It seems quite likely that Carol became involved in other "affairs" in the last 12 months of her life, and may well have been engaged in one in July 1976. There is, however, no evidence of any "suitor" at this time and, if there was one, he remains unidentified and is unlikely therefore to have needed or wanted to embark on an elaborate murder and body concealment plan, even if he had a motive for killing Carol.

It should be very obvious by now that there could only be one man "in the frame" for the murder. One man who had a likely motive, the opportunity and all the facility, resources and skills that other potential suspects would almost certainly have lacked. Add to the mix the fact that the body was clothed in a nightie, Gordon Park's character, his propensity for planning, detail and meticulousness and his conduct in the days and weeks after 17 July 1976, and you surely have the only candidate for the deed. It would also surely be in the mind of the jury that most murders are "domestic", husband on wife or vice versa. There must have been no evidence or circumstances in this case that would have remotely displaced this likelihood here.

I pedalled my views on the evidence, and those of my immediate colleagues and the police, relentlessly to my superiors but they fell on stony ground. My last hope was that leading counsel, who was to be asked to consider the case and advise, would take a different view to the senior CPS personnel. As it turned out, this was a forlorn hope.

I had wanted to brief a Queen's Counsel of repute and considerable criminal case experience to consider the evidence, and I had hoped that we could instruct Brian Leveson, who had recently prosecuted the notorious Rosemary West. Sadly, he was not available and somehow we ended up with a venerable QC from chambers in Manchester called Jack Price, who, I confess, I had never heard of before this time. Be that as it may, I prepared a brief for him and on 19 December 1997, Phil Bates and I, together with the senior police investigators and David Farmer, Mike Graham's deputy, met Jack Price in conference at his chambers.

Prior to the conference I had heard a rumour that CPS senior management had already been in telephone contact with Jack Price and communicated their views that there was not a realistic prospect of conviction in the case. This tended to be borne out by a copy of a memo I later came across that had been sent by our office in Carlisle, clearly on senior management instructions, and without my knowledge or connivance. This memo asserted that "Mr Price should be aware that the views of both the... Mr Graham... and Mr Farmer are that there is not a realistic prospect of conviction in this matter." This was presumably designed to counter any different view that I might have set out in the brief to counsel, and also to "guide" counsel on the sort of advice we were expecting him to give. He did not disappoint and his views on the case mirrored those of Mike Graham and David Farmer

A Very Cumbrian Murder

and came up with much the same reasoning as Mike had previously set out in his own review of the case.

The only slightly surprising difference was that, in the conference, Jack Price had indicated that he did not think the delay and the fact of the missing file from 1976 presented a great problem. In his later written advice to us, however, he had reverted to the opinion that these circumstances provided the defence with a strong argument that that the case should be "stayed" as an "abuse of process". A rather unconvincing "volte-face"!

There was essentially no resistance to counsel's views in the conference and no attempt to present contrary views. As the police, Phil Bates and I knew what David Farmer's views were, it would have been inappropriate to express contrary opinions and, certainly as far as Phil and I were concerned, there was the principle of "collective responsibility" on the part of the CPS to be observed. My stance in the conference therefore was to make no contribution at all and let the proceedings take their inevitable course!

All that remained was for the "last rites" to be administered to the case and, early in the new year I issued a formal notice of discontinuance of the proceedings against Gordon Park, on the grounds of "insufficient evidence". This would not prevent us from resurrecting the case if new material evidence was to come to light, but my own depressing view was that this was most unlikely. Fortunately, I was to be proved wrong…

Chapter Nine

Proceedings Revisited: Re-charge, Trial and Appeal (1998 to 2010)

The national newspapers had been drawn to the case from the moment that Carol's body was recovered from Coniston Water. The investigating officers had christened it "The Lady in the Lake", after the 1943 novel of the same name by Raymond Chandler – hardly original, but, bearing as it did the aura of dark, romantic, Arthurian legend, it was almost guaranteed to attract the attention of the wider media. The discontinuance of the case in early 1998 was the cue for a welter of publicity for the case in all the main daily and Sunday newspapers, and a couple of television documentaries followed in due course. Gordon himself gave an interview to a freelance journalist and the ensuing article appeared in the Mail on Sunday.

When interviewed by the police in 2004, Gordon maintained that he was a very reluctant interviewee, and that he found all the press and TV coverage sensationalised and not entirely accurate, and this included the article to which he had himself contributed. He stated, however, that he had been advised by his solicitor to give one interview to a selected journalist, in order to put an end to the harassment he was getting from the press at large, all of whom were anxious to talk to him and print his story. For his "pains" he was paid the sum of

£50,000 by the Mail on Sunday, which must have gone some way to ease his discomfort!

Otherwise there is no evidence that Gordon benefitted financially in any other way from Carol's death. In his 2004 interviews with the police he stressed that he did not receive any income or capital from any pension plan she may have had, and there was no return from any insurance policy on her life, and in fact he had not sought to look for any such benefits.

As far as his everyday existence is concerned, Gordon returned to married life with Jennifer, pursuing various shared interests such as cycling – they both joined a tandem-riding club at some point. According to Gordon, however, he gave up his great passion of sailing after 1997. He claimed that he thought it would be "inappropriate" to carry on sailing boats, particularly on Coniston Water, after Carol's body had been recovered. There is documentary evidence that Gordon had a mooring on Windermere until at least 1985; and a member of Coniston Sailing Club in the 1980s knew Gordon as a fellow-member at this time and that he had a mooring at the south end of Coniston Water, preferring to be here rather than nearer the sailing club as "it was more secluded". There is, however, no evidence to contradict Gordon's assertion that he ceased to be an active sailor after 1997.

★ ★ ★

Although the intensive investigation was over, the police continued, albeit in a much more low-key fashion, to keep the case under review and pursue various lines of enquiry. Detective Superintendent Ian Douglas had made it plain in a press release, after the charge was dropped, that the case "was not closed" and the investigation would continue. Whilst I am fairly sure that all the investigative team clearly believed that Park was the only suspect, it would have been improper for the police to have publicly announced that they 'were not looking for anyone else', and indeed there were some inquiries made in 1998 into the possibility of a third party in Spain being involved in the murder, an inquiry, however, that revealed no useful evidence.

Closer to home, in the summer of 2000 the police investigative team revealed the early results of another, seemingly more fruitful, line of enquiry. They had tracked down and hired another knot expert called Michael Lucas. Mr Lucas was an independent knot expert with over 40 years of experience in his field. He had an impressive list of qualifications including membership of the International Guild of Knot Tyers, the world-wide forum for knot experts and other exponents of knotting. Over the previous nine years he had given evidence as an expert witness in a number of criminal trials and coroners' inquests using his knowledge of knots and cordage. He had now been asked to examine the knots and ropes connected to the body, and also the ropes and cords recovered from Gordon's two homes and material found in boats owned by him, and to further develop, if possible, the findings of the original 'knots expert', Roger Ide.

Mr Lucas presented his initial findings at a meeting on 17 August 2000 attended by senior police officers, and also by Phil Bates and David Farmer, who was now the chief crown prosecutor for Cumbria (the CPS North area having ceased to exist in April 1999). I was not present at the meeting but it seems that the potential evidence that Mr Lucas could give was promising and might take Roger

Ide's conclusions a stage further and, indeed, to a point where reviving the criminal proceedings might be a realistic prospect. The downside at this time was that there would be a substantial cost involved in Mr Lucas refining and finalising his research, and there was some uncertainty as to whether the police could justify the expense of this and also generally continuing the investigation.

Almost two years would pass before the CPS would learn that the investigation was still very much alive and that, indeed, yet more material evidence had been acquired by the investigators. In April 2002 David Farmer was contacted by Detective Chief Inspector Keith Churchman, who was now the senior investigating officer in the case, and invited to arrange a meeting to discuss some new evidence that had been acquired, together with that of Mr Lucas.

The meeting took place in the summer of 2002, attended by DCI Churchman, Detective Inspector McBride and Detective Sergeant Doug Marshall on the police side; and David Farmer, Phil Bates and myself from the CPS. Ian McBride was on the verge of retirement from the police service, and by strange coincidence was the name Gordon Park was to identify in his 2004 police interviews as someone whose name he had been given as a person with whom Carol had associated during her marriage. He could not, however, provide the source of his information and conceded it was just hearsay and "tittle-tattle". Doug Marshall had been heavily involved in the 1997 investigation and represented a point of continuity between the earlier enquiry and the continuing investigation.

Although it was two years since Michael Lucas had given his presentation, it did not seem that his own investigation was yet complete and his final report was still awaited. There were, however, we learnt, two new statements now in existence which provided a whole new source of material evidence. Michael Wainwright had been in Preston prison with Gordon Park during the time that the latter was remanded in custody in August and September 1997. We were told that Wainwright had contacted the police in September 2000 and informed them that Park had told him that he had killed his wife. He had come forward after seeing a Channel 4 TV programme in which the murder of Carol Park had featured. Wainwright had made a formal witness statement in October 2000 setting out Park's 'confession' to him, and he also gave the police details of other prisoners who had been in the prison at the same time as Park. One of those persons, Glen Banks from Blackburn, had been traced and interviewed on video, and he too, had claimed that Park had told him that he had murdered his wife. We were told that his account was by no means identical to that of Wainwright, but that it appeared to the investigators that the two of them had had no contact with each other since they had left prison.

On the face of it this was a very important development, providing direct evidence of Park's responsibility for the murder. It certainly was sufficient for David Farmer to agree that it would justify Park's re-arrest and for the criminal proceedings to be revived. The decision taken at the meeting was that we would meet again when Mr Lucas had submitted his final report, only this time with leading counsel present.

A Very Cumbrian Murder

This meeting did not take place for another 18 months, and the time that the investigation had taken since the discontinuance of the earlier prosecution was to prove a matter of concern for counsel when he came to advise on the issue of the case being resurrected. Fortunately, the delay was not to prove fatal to the success of the case.

★ ★ ★

It was 16 December 2003 when the crucial case conference with leading counsel took place. Those attending included the members of the police investigative team and David Farmer, Phil Bates and myself from the CPS side. Michael Lucas joined us for the morning session. The important development was that the conference was attended by newly-instructed leading counsel. Alistair Webster QC, from Lincoln House Chambers in Manchester, was well-known to Phil Bates and myself as he had recently prosecuted a couple of high profile cases from Cumbria, and was an established, robust and highly competent counsel.

The morning session was largely given over to Mr Lucas presenting his report and providing a practical demonstration of knot tying.

Commenting on Park's admissions in police interviews in 1997 as to the range of knots he was able to tie, Mr Lucas took the view that he was in the category of a "knot enthusiast". The skills professed by Park were, said Mr Lucas, beyond the range of knots commonly used by the average small boat sailor. The latter would be able to tie no more than about eight different knots whereas Park had listed some 15 knots and splices with which he was familiar.

As far as the knots used on the body were concerned, Mr Lucas stated that they were appropriate for the purpose, well tied and were clearly intended to provide a strong durable form of packaging that would resist the ravages of many years under water.

Comparing knots on the body and body packaging with knots found elsewhere, but attributable to Park, Mr Lucas found examples in both categories of locations of unusual use of stopper knots, correctly-tied bowlines, extensive use of overhand loops to make lashings more secure, a similar manner of forming eye-splices and associated heat-sealing and confident use of loop-type knots. The use of stopper knots in particular seemed to indicate "an involuntary habit, which is unusual amongst yachtsmen, although sometimes used by climbers as extra security".

The conclusion that Mr Lucas had expressed in his report and which he initially confirmed in the conference was that the knots on the body and those at the other locations were tied by the same person. He was able to draw this conclusion by virtue of the large number of clearly identifiable knot comparisons, and because of the unusually high level of skill displayed in the selection and use of the knots on the body bindings, almost all of which were named by Park as within his knowledge and capacity to tie.

If that conclusion was valid and sustainable, then, if the reader will excuse the rather inappropriate metaphor, Gordon Park was 'dead in the water'. The point was, however, that it was not valid and sustainable, and, under questioning by counsel, Mr Lucas conceded that he could not rule out the possibility that some person other than the defendant could have been responsible for tying the knots on the body. Counsel invited him to rephrase his conclusion using the range of findings typically used by the Forensic Science Service in such circumstances, and he now maintained that it would be more accurate to say that there was "extremely strong support" for the proposition that the defendant was responsible for tying the knots on the body. In an amended statement Mr Lucas produced a week later, he had diluted this conclusion to one of "very strong support".

After Mr Lucas had departed, the conference went on to consider the statement of Michael Wainwright and the video interview of Glen Banks.

Michael Wainwright, a native of west Lancashire, had been sentenced to six months' imprisonment on 27 August 1997 for breaching the requirements of a probation order, which had been imposed for an offence of assault on a child under the age of 14. Wainwright was sent initially to Preston prison to serve his sentence, and, like Park, was placed on F Wing, which was specifically for 'protected prisoners'. Within a few days he was introduced to Glen Banks, and learnt that Banks' cell mate was Gordon Park. He maintains that at this stage he did not know why Park was a prisoner.

According to Wainwright, Banks told him that he "wasn't getting enough sleep", because Park was constantly talking in his sleep about the "Lake Coniston murder". Having established that Park was facing a murder charge, Wainwright says that he started to take an interest in him. He wasn't, he says, a typical primary school teacher, and "he had an evil look in his eyes". Other prisoners used to shout at Park in the exercise yard, "Bin Bags" being a common term used. Wainwright claimed that this affected Park, who then used to retreat to a corner, where he would start "mumbling". Wainwright states that he heard one mumbled remark to the effect that "she deserved it".

After he'd been in the prison for about a week, Wainwright says that he managed to engage Park in conversation. Park, he claims, began to talk about the murder and made what amounted to a confession to him. Park told him that he "didn't want to do it" but "she shouldn't have done what she did to me, seeing other people instead of being reliable to me". He then went on to tell Wainwright that he had put his hands round his wife's neck until she lost consciousness, and then hit her with an axe. According to Wainwright, Park described the axe as black-handled with a metal shaft, with a pick on one side and an axe on the other. Wainwright recognised the description because he had used the same sort of axe when he had been rock-climbing. After hitting her with the axe, he says that Park told him the body was placed in his car and then taken to his boat and then "she had gone down".

Wainwright states that at this point he felt "physically sick" and was unable to sleep at night. Nonetheless he had subsequent conversations with Park, but not about the murder. In particular, he recalls asking Park to help him with a Politics course he was undertaking but Park declined because he was "only a primary school teacher". Shortly after this Park did not return from a court hearing and Wainwright did not see him again.

Wainwright decided not to tell anyone about Park's confession. He was worried, he says, that Park "may send someone" to his home, and he tried to put the whole incident out of his mind. But then in September 2000 he saw a TV documentary on Channel Four about Lake

A Very Cumbrian Murder

District murders, one of which was the murder of Carol Park. At the end of the programme there was an appeal from Carol's relatives for help to catch the killer. This, he said, revived all his old memories and he spent a sleepless night. He then disclosed what he knew to his girlfriend and his father, and the latter advised him to ring the police.

Glen Banks was also serving a sentence in Preston prison at the time of Park's remand time there, and he says that Park was his cell mate on F Wing for about four days. During this period, Banks fell into conversation with Park, and he maintains that over about two days Park disclosed that he had murdered his wife and how he had done it. Park told him that he and his wife were celebrating an anniversary on Park's boat, which was on "some sort of boating lake". The children had been left "without a babysitter". They had an argument on the boat and Park had put "some white powder" in his wife's drink, whereupon she "became sleepy". Park then went on to tell him that he had put his wife in a black bag with weights in it to weigh the body down. The "body" was then put over the side of the boat. Park then went home to his children and the next day took them to Blackpool.

Park, he says, told him not to tell anyone. He had since never heard anything about the Park case, had not seen any TV programme about it, and, because of his reading difficulties did not look at newspapers.

There was also a statement from a social worker, Yvonne Quinn, who had worked with Banks since August 1999. Glen, she said, lived in supported tenancy accommodation in Blackburn. He had a learning disability, and there were "some areas in life that he does not function as he might do". She was, however, present during the video interview of Banks and her opinion was, from her experience of him, that "I had no reason to doubt the information he provided to the police was genuine".

When he was interviewed by the police in January 2004, Gordon Park, maintained that the name "Wainwright" meant nothing to him, other than being that of the eminent walker and author, Alfred Wainwright. He had, he said, never spoken to anyone of that name at the prison, and the only prisoner he had been in a position to help was his cell mate Banks, whom he assisted to write a letter to his mother. Park said that he used to keep his own company in the exercise yard and was not routinely abused by other inmates. He was unaware that he had been given any nickname. The suggestion that he retreated to a corner and mumbled was absolute "fantasy", as was the whole "confession" attributed to him by Wainwright. He had been advised by his solicitor not to discuss the case with anyone whilst in prison, he said, and this was advice that he had heeded.

As far as Banks was concerned, Park stated that he was "inadequate" and barely literate. He learnt that he had been bullied previously. Because they were confined together, he made an effort to get on with him and may have given him some basic personal details about his family and where he was from, but did not at any time discuss the case with him.

Park maintained that everyone on the wing knew why he was there –"it was all over the TV". The fact that Carol had been involved in affairs was on the television, and the Blackpool trip was "common knowledge".

I have to say that I was far from convinced that Banks and Wainwright were truthful witnesses. The arguments in their favour were that they had nothing to gain by inventing their respective stories, that there was no evidence that they had colluded before their "disclosures" and that they had given their accounts independently of each other, and that they were giving what amounted to versions of events that tended to match the known or inferred facts, facts that they could only have learnt from the perpetrator of the crime. For me, however, this was as good as it got, and the case for their evidence being authentic was outweighed by the case against.

In the first place, the evidence of 'prison snitches' must always be treated with caution, since they may have some oblique motive for inventing their accounts. The trial judge would have had to direct the jury in such terms. Both Banks and Wainwright were also, of course, convicted criminals. All this is not to say that they were not capable of telling the truth, but it does mean that what they say has to be carefully scrutinised.

What motives might they have had for coming forward with an invented story? There is no evidence that they received any financial reward for what they did, but, there again, certainly in the case of Wainwright, awareness that the case had attracted national publicity and that no culprit had been brought to book may have engendered hopes or expectations that some kind of reward may have been forthcoming. There is, of course, also the proposition that persons whose lives are humdrum and uneventful, or have been studded with petty crime or misfortune, may have relished the opportunity of briefly stepping into the limelight and basking in the glare of publicity.

In this connection, Banks is in a slightly different position from Wainwright as he claims that he did not know of the media publicity when he was approached by the police. This, of course, may well not be true, but if it is, it may appear on the face of it that his story is gratuitous and without selfish motive, and, moreover, without knowledge that Wainwright had already provided his account or what it contained. A spontaneous and unsolicited tale no less?! What we don't know, however, is what was said by the police investigators to Banks before he was interviewed on video. How did they encourage him to tell his story? What information did they give him? Was he told what Wainwright had told them, that Banks was the source of tales of Park's mutterings in his sleep? It seems unlikely that Banks would simply 'come out with it', not without some kind of prompting from his questioners. Nor can we be certain that Banks and Wainwright had never met since their release from Preston prison, and discussed the case. Both of them, of course, lived in Lancashire.

What about the content of their respective accounts? Wainwright's story is the more plausible of the two, and may well be close to what actually happened to Carol at the hands of Gordon Park. It must be the case, therefore, it is said, that he acquired this account from Park himself. That, however, would be a much more acceptable proposition if there had never been any media publicity about the case in the three years between the recovery of Carol's body and Wainwright coming forward in 2000. Whilst, in theory at least, there are restrictions on media publicity about a criminal case between a person being charged and his trial, there is nothing to stop the press and TV broadcasting masses of detail before and after this period. There was a good deal of news coverage from the

A Very Cumbrian Murder

moment the body was pulled out of Coniston Water, and reams of press, and later TV, coverage from the time the case was dropped. At one time or another, Wainwright could have easily picked up all the details of the description of the murder which he claims he got from the mouth of Park himself.

Banks' account is much less plausible. He makes no reference to any murder weapon, and the notion that the Parks would leave the children unattended whilst out "celebrating" an anniversary on a boat, and that Park would have covertly provided himself beforehand with a drug and a black bag and weights, seems fanciful to say the least. Again, such details as might match the 'facts' could easily have been gleaned from early or later publicity or even, it seems, from gossip and 'tittle-tattle' on the prison wing.

The two accounts, moreover, are markedly different in several important respects. If Park had 'confessed' to two persons in a short space of time, why would he give them different versions? Banks also makes no reference to any sleep-talking by Park, and he seems to be saying that he never told anyone else about what he'd been told by Park.

It is fair to say that Banks comes across quite well in the video interview. But then at the trial he changed his story more than once and even claimed that the killing took place whilst the Parks were actually sailing to Blackpool. It was put to him that he was "highly suggestible". This seems to be a distinct possibility.

Wainwright, at the trial, acknowledged being a heavy cannabis smoker and admitted to "hearing voices". He also added to his story by claiming that Park told him that he had gone upstairs and found Carol in bed with another man and killed her in a fit of rage (*Bluestones* is a bungalow!).

Then we must consider why Gordon Park would have made such 'confessions'. Why would a man of obviously stern composure, who had 'stone-walled' his way through a series of interviews with experienced detectives, suddenly make unsolicited admissions of guilt to complete strangers? No doubt he would have been at a low ebb in prison and perhaps he was lured into a false sense of security by believing that he was 'amongst friends' and that his secret was safe with them! Hardly likely, surely. It would have been totally out of character and a complete departure from the steely and unbending character that we have come to know, if not to love. Does it seem likely that he would bare his soul to Glen Banks, a person he regarded as a half-wit? A 'cell mate' perhaps, but hardly a 'soul-mate'! And doesn't Park's statement that he kept himself to himself in the exercise yard have the ring of truth? He would have nothing in common with most of his fellow inmates, and certainly not with a man like Wainwright. Why would he fraternise with such a character, let alone make a confession of murder to him?

Despite my reservations, which I did not voice in any event at the conference, counsel found the evidence of Banks and Wainwright believable and convincing (or so he said in his written opinion given later!) and was in no doubt that this evidence, coupled with that of Mr Lucas, fully justified Park being re-arrested and the proceedings against him being resurrected. I was not going to argue with this, and neither was anyone else!

Counsel also considered the issue of delay in the case and that of the missing 1976 police file, matters which had

A Very Cumbrian Murder

troubled Jack Price QC in 1997. Alistair Webster had no real worries about these issues, bearing in mind that the real cause of the delay was the deliberate secretion of the body, allegedly, of course, by Gordon Park. What was of more concern to counsel, however, was the delay since 1998, occasioned by the apparently leisurely pace of the police investigation since that date. The tardiness of the inquiry was highlighted by the fact that the evidence of Wainwright was available in 2000, that of Banks in 2002 and that of Mr Lucas as early as 1999. DCI Churchman did have an explanation for the delay, mainly based on the limited police resources to carry out the further investigation and the need for the police to prioritise their many enquiries. Despite his concern, counsel was not convinced that Park would be able to show, in all the circumstances, that the delay had caused him such prejudice that there could not be a fair trial, and he remained strongly of the opinion that the case should be pursued to re-arrest, re-charge and sent to trial.

And so it was that early on the morning of 13 January 2004, police officers went once again to 34 Norland Avenue, and there re-arrested Gordon Park on suspicion of the murder of his then wife on or about 17 July 1976...

★ ★ ★

Following his arrest, the police once again made a search of Park's home address, and once again seized quantities of ropes, cords and string from the house and outbuildings. An ice axe was also seized from the garage.

The defendant was interviewed, again at great length, by various of the investigating officers, between 13 and 15 January. Much of these interviews focused on his time in prison custody in 1997 and conversations he was alleged to have had with Michael Wainwright and Glen Banks. How he responded to this line of questioning, we have already seen.

He was also quizzed at length about his experience and expertise with knots, and he was confronted with the findings and opinion of Mr Lucas. He accepted that the knots on all the ropes, cords and string recovered by the police, now and in 1997, were almost certainly tied by him, and that they bore examples of bowlines, granny knots, reef knots, various hitches, overhand knots, sheet bends, figure-of-eight knots and eyesplices, and also examples of the heat-sealing the ends of ropes. He agreed that he would often use figure-of-eight knot as "stopper" knots, as a "belt and braces" approach in case other knots above it should slip or fail. He would use granny knots for this purpose as well. He had learnt how to tie most of these knots and the eye splice in the scouts, and other knots he had picked up as a rock climber, going on to use them all in his sailing activities. He denied, however, that he was responsible for tying the knots on the body, and also that he had a "habit" of regularly using stopper knots – sometimes he used them and sometimes he did not.

He agreed that the ice axe recovered was his. He stated that it was the only one he had ever owned and pointed out that it had a wooden, not a metal, shaft. It wouldn't have been used in connection with rock-climbing, but, as Park told the officers, only on snow and ice, for which it was designed.

The officers also revisited with Park the period immediately before Carol's final disappearance in 1976. Park insisted that he had no suspicion or cause to suspect that Carol was associating with any other man at that time. Since 1997, however, he had been told that there were

A Very Cumbrian Murder

such persons at that time, and he had been told specifically about two such men, one being a Barrow solicitor called Gordon Nuttall and another a local police officer called McBride. It had also been suggested to him that there were others in this period. He could not, however, name the source of this information and stressed that it was "hearsay and tittle-tattle".

The interviews did not advance the case against Park any further than the evidence which had already been gathered, and it was almost inevitable that he was going to be re-charged with Carol's murder whatever he said in those interviews, unless he had come up with some compelling reason to the contrary. Thus, following the final interview on 15 January 2004, Gordon Park was once again charged with the murder of Carol Park on or about 17 July 1976. He made no reply to the charge.

★ ★ ★

As it turned out, there was more evidence to come, in the form of an alleged "eyewitness" to a man dumping a package in the lake from a boat, and also some physical evidence from Coniston Water itself.

Joan Young, who lived in Scotland, contacted the police in Barrow in January 2004. She and her husband had been regular summer visitors to Keswick since the early 1970s. She told the police that she was always able to be very specific about dates, and recalled that they came to Keswick in the hot summer of 1976, arriving in the town on 25 July. She also had a particular recollection of that summer holiday because her husband had sustained a torn cartilage and was walking with the aid of crutches. She remembered that two or three days into their stay they drove out to Hawkshead and thence down the east side of

Coniston Water, stopping at a designated parking place about halfway down the lake.

Whilst sat in the car, and after a short while, Mrs Young says she noticed a white boat out on the lake. It had a mast but was not displaying sails, and had one male occupant. Out of "general interest" she watched the boat through binoculars for some little time. The lone sailor was standing up in the boat and she could see that he was slim, with brown or auburn hair, and was wearing glasses. She then saw him pick up a bulky item from the bottom of the boat, similar to a "rolled up carpet", and then push the item into the water. The item appeared to sink. Mrs Young's husband was also watching the spectacle and Mrs Young recalls that she was moved to comment to him that "perhaps he's getting rid of his wife". A flippant remark, but perhaps one of great significance.

The Youngs left the scene shortly afterwards, but Mrs Young was sufficiently intrigued by what she had witnessed to check newspapers and news bulletins for some weeks after the incident, although she did not, at this time, think it worth reporting to the police.

More than 20 years later, in 1998, the Youngs were again in Keswick and in a hotel bar Mrs Young noticed a newspaper cutting on the wall relating to the case of the "Lady in the Lake" and the dead body recovered from Coniston Water. From reading the article she formed the impression that the person who had been charged in the case had been found "Not Guilty" and so she saw no point in informing the police of what she had seen in 1976. That was not the end of the matter, however, because in January 2004 Mrs Young's sister phoned her to tell her about a man having been re-arrested for a murder involving a body in Coniston Water, and this time Mrs

Young did get in touch with the police. Before she made a formal witness statement she actually saw a picture of Gordon Park in an article about the case on the internet, and was "sure" that this was the man she had seen in the boat on the lake in 1976.

In the event, the trial judge would not allow the evidence of Mrs Young's 'identification' of Gordon Park as the man in the boat to go before the jury. This is perhaps not altogether surprising. The photograph that she had seen on the internet was of a man nearly 30 years older than the man she had seen in 1976, a man she had only seen at a distance through a pair of binoculars. Such evidence was considered too weak and unreliable to be allowed to stand, its prejudicial effect outweighing its probative value. It also has to be considered, of course, that it would have been very tempting for Mrs Young to be "sure" of her identification when she was aware that the man on the internet was the person who had been arrested and charged!

So that left Mrs Young's testimony as another piece in the 'jigsaw' of circumstantial evidence upon which the case against Gordon Park was largely based, leaving aside, of course, the 'confession' evidence of Messrs Banks and Wainwright.

So how strong, and how probative of Park's guilt, was her evidence? She is recalling events that had occurred some 28 years before. Can she be certain about the year, let alone the month? If one accepts the accuracy of her recollection, then what she describes must have taken place some 11 or 12 days after Carol is last seen and was almost certainly murdered. Would Park have waited so long to dispose of the body and then done it in broad daylight?

On the other hand, what the Youngs saw that day is very probably exactly what was done to dispose of Carol Park's body. It represents a remarkable coincidence and it makes Mrs Young's comment at the time to her husband extraordinarily prescient! Her description of the man in the boat is not that distant from Park's appearance at that time. At his trial, Park initially claimed that he did not wear glasses outside the house in 1976, but, when shown a photograph of him taken in 1973 wearing spectacles in such a setting, he concedes he is clearly mistaken about this. He also maintained, when giving evidence, that although the 505 dinghy he had owned was masted and was also white in colour, he had sold it in June 1976 and did not in fact have a boat in July. He agreed, however, that his sailing log showed the sale as being in July 1976. It will be recalled that Colin Smith says he was regularly crewing for Gordon in the 505 dinghy at this time.

The physical evidence which was recovered in 2004 was either of dubious origin or was of no great value. A stone retrieved from the lake bed near to where the body was found matched the stones found in one of the walls of *Bluestones*. The stone was not indigenous to Coniston Water and the inference therefore would have been that it had been taken by Gordon from his home to weigh the body down. The problem, however, was that the stone in question had apparently been recovered by a diving team in 1997, but only examined and considered as potential evidence in 2004, and the prosecution faced difficulties at the trial in establishing that the item had actually been on the lake bed and recovered from there. There was a problem in establishing the provenance of the item which, in effect, undermined the value of the evidence.

A Very Cumbrian Murder

There was also a piece of Westmoreland slate recovered from the lake bed in the vicinity of the location of the body, again something that would not normally be found in Coniston Water. This matched the slate on the roof of *Bluestones*. This type of slate, however, had been worked in the area for hundreds of years and, thus, could have come from anywhere in the locality. This piece of evidence therefore was of only very limited value, even as part of the circumstantial case against the defendant.

★ ★ ★

After he had been re-charged, the case against Gordon Park moved slowly but surely towards the inevitable trial. The case papers were prepared by the prosecution team and served upon the defence, and a good deal of material which had been gathered by the police during the investigations in 1997 and in the ensuing years but which did not form part of the evidential case against the defendant was also disclosed to the defence team. Park appeared in the Crown Court, where he was arraigned (ie. the charge put to him and a plea invited). To no-one's surprise Gordon pleaded "Not Guilty" and in due course a trial date of 22 November 2004 was set. The trial was to take place at Manchester Crown Court and was estimated to take about ten weeks. There was almost 11 months between Park being charged and the start of his trial, but this was by no means unusual in a case of this seriousness and with a potentially large number of witnesses. Another year in the life of a case which had its origins in events which had taken place nearly 30 years ago was hardly going to make much difference in the overall scheme of things. The defendant, moreover, was not languishing in prison throughout this period, the prosecution having conceded from the outset that it was not appropriate to oppose bail, bearing in mind of course that he had fully complied with his bail conditions in 1997.

As well as considering the additional pieces of evidence that emerged in 2004, the prosecution team met on a number of occasions to discuss various aspects of the case and to formulate strategy for its presentation to the jury. The pathologist, Dr Tapp, attended one of these conferences and let it be known that he considered that the deceased's injuries were more likely to have been inflicted with a small hand axe, with a sharp edge and a blunt edge, than an unwieldy climber's ice axe. No such implement was ever recovered, but then Park would have had plenty of time to have disposed of it.

Another more significant development was the decision taken, close to the trial date, by leading counsel, effectively to ditch Michael Lucas, or at least any part of his evidence where he expressed opinions about the authorship of the knots on the body. The other 'knot expert', Roger Ide, had seen Lucas' reports, and, whilst conceding that Lucas was more experienced in commenting on boating knots than himself, was quite disparaging about much of the other man's evidence. He pointed out a number of factual errors in Lucas' reports, and did not accept some of the latter's conclusions. When challenged, Mr Lucas tended to become flustered, and he was now further downgrading his opinion that his findings provided "very strong support" for the proposition that the same person had tied the knots on the body and those on the recovered cordage attributable to Park to one of just "strong support". Alistair Webster had by now come to the conclusion that Mr Lucas as a witness would prove to be "flaky" and could well be undermined in cross-examination, to the detriment of the prosecution case as a whole. Four years of reliance on the 'expertise.' of the hapless Michael Lucas therefore came to a sad end!

★ ★ ★

The first three and a half days of the trial were taken up with prelimary matters and legal argument. In this time, the judge was persuaded by the defence to exclude the evidence of Joan Young relating to the identification of Gordon Park, for the reasons cited above. The defence also sought to have the evidence of Wainwright and Banks ruled out, on the basis that it would be unfair for this evidence to be led when prison records were missing, records which would have shown whether they were actually in Preston prison at the same time as Park and if so, on which wing. This evidence was particularly important, said defence counsel, as far as Wainwright was concerned because Park denied that he knew or had ever met him. The judge, however, did not see that the missing records could create unfairness and he ruled that the evidence should be allowed and he would deal with the situation by appropriate warnings to the jury.

As expected, the defence also argued that it would be an abuse of process of the court for the trial to go ahead. This was based on two grounds:

1) The original Missing Person file had never been found and it was apparent that it contained material evidence that might have been beneficial to the defence – such as the statements made in 1997 by David Brearley and Sabrine Dixon. The loss of that evidence was potentially prejudicial to the defendant's ability to have a fair trial.

2) The delay between the dropping of the first case and the defendant being re-charged was "unexplained and

inexplicable". Further, the additional evidence that had been acquired in this period by the police was not very substantial, now that Lucas was not being relied upon, and there was no real reason why the trial could not have taken place three years ago. This delay only served to compound the original delay of 21 years and meant that the evidence had become that much more stale, and again this prejudiced the chances of a fair trial.

The judge rejected these submissions. In the first place he said that to stop the trial on the grounds of an "abuse of process" would only happen in exceptional circumstances, and even if there had been delay which is unjustified, the application would only succeed if there was serious prejudice to the prospects of a fair trial. He agreed with prosecuting counsel that the delay between 1997 and 2004 was not inordinate and certainly not sufficient to cause that sort of prejudice. As far as the missing file was concerned, he said that the witnesses referred to by defence counsel were still available to give evidence, and thus again there was no serious prejudice to the defendant's entitlement to a fair trial. Finally, the judge stated that, in any event, these issues could be dealt with in the trial process itself, by him giving appropriate directions to the jury in due course.

No great surprises in any of the judge's rulings and the decks were now cleared and the trial proper was ready to start, which it did on the morning of 25 November with a jury being 'sworn in'. Prosecuting counsel then outlined the Crown's case to the jury. The first witness, Ivor Price, began to give his evidence the same afternoon.

★ ★ ★

A Very Cumbrian Murder

So, at the start of the trial in the case of Regina versus Gordon Park, what was the Crown's case? How did it differ from it would have been if the trial had commenced in 1998? What was the strength, if any, of the evidence that had been gathered since that time?

As far as I was concerned the case as it stood in 1998 was the case. Of the additional evidence, the much-vaunted opinions of Michael Lucas had been abandoned. The "geological evidence" was either dubious or inconsequential. The testimony of Joan Young, shorn now of its claim to identify the defendant, was useful, but only formed part of the general circumstantial case against Park. The "jailhouse snitch" evidence of Messrs Banks and Wainwright, as I saw it anyway, was flawed, inconsistent, and highly suspicious. I believe there was some consensus that the sworn evidence of Banks at the trial was "plausible", but it is interesting, perhaps, that when three judges at the Court of Appeal in November 2008 rejected Park's appeal against conviction, they ruled that the new evidence that Park's counsel was seeking to have introduced did not raise "a reasonable doubt as to the safety of this conviction" and that there was a "strong circumstantial case against the defendant". Its back to that phrase again – "strong circumstantial case" and no reference to prison confessions or rocks on the lake bed. It is also interesting that Alistair Webster, albeit in a giveaway remark, had at one stage commented that, had he been instructed counsel in 1998, he would have been inclined to want to pursue the case as it stood then.

Although he clearly referred to the Banks/Wainwright "confessions" and the geological evidence in presenting the prosecution case to the jury, the real thrust of the way in which the case was delivered by Alistair Webster was the compelling nature of the circumstantial evidence. Thus, in his opening address to the jury, he encapsulated the prosecution's position in this passage:

"Whoever killed and disposed of Carol Park would have the following characteristics: a person who knew her sufficiently well to come across her in her short nightdress; a person who had reason to strongly dislike her or lose his temper with her; a person who was thoroughly familiar with knots, both as a sailor and a climber; a meticulous person; a person with access to a boat and familiarity with Coniston Water. One man fits this description: Gordon Park."

The elaborate and sophisticated way in which the body was disposed of, and the place in which it was concealed, ruled out murder by a "secret lover or a mysterious stranger".

All the other pieces of evidence which go towards supporting the proposition above, and which are rehearsed in chapter eight and elsewhere in this book were advanced in the course of the prosecution case at the trial: the likely tight time-frame in which the murder was carried out, particularly bearing in mind that Carol had evinced no intention to leave her home and children at this time and that there was no reliable evidence that she was ever seen alive again after 16 July 1976; Park's conduct in the days and weeks immediately following this date; the evidence of his character – manipulative, controlling, obsessive, meticulous – from both his first and second marriages; his conduct on being made aware that Carol's body had been recovered.

Over the ten weeks of the trial that followed, many of the witnesses whose accounts have been referred to previously in this book, gave their evidence on oath. Park

A Very Cumbrian Murder

himself gave sworn evidence on his own behalf and persisted in his insistence that he was not the killer of his first wife. His evidence deviated very little from the accounts he had given in interview with the police in 1997 and 2004. There were, however, a few matters that could be highlighted:

1) Although he had denied this in 1997, Park now admitted that he had taken Carol to the High Duddon guesthouse in 1974. Cross-examined about this, he denied that he had changed his story because he had been made aware of the evidence of the Walkers. There was, he said, no crisis at this time – she merely wanted time on her own, to "sort out her own thoughts". There was no mention at this point of another man and it wasn't until she rang him at school on 26 September that she said that she wanted a divorce. He didn't learn about David Brearley until just before Christmas that year, when he also found out that she planned to go and live with him.

2) He admitted that he had lied to the probation officer Anne Hollows and to the magistrates' court in Teesside about his relationship with Judith Walmsley, when he had claimed that their relationship was not an intimate one. He now said that it was a full physical relationship, but he had not wanted to disclose this at the time because he had felt that it might jeopardise his prospects of being awarded custody of the children.

3) Regarding the trip to Blackpool on 17 July 1976, Park now said that he did not recall seeing Carol that morning, but he knew that she didn't want to go on the trip (in interview in 1997 he has said that he had left her in bed). In cross-examination he stated that Carol had been "looking forward to it". She made some "light excuse" for not wanting to go. She wasn't ill, however. He

couldn't recall what he said to Ivan Price about her reason for not wanting to go. He maintained that it would have been "most unusual" for the children not to have seen their mother that morning. There was nothing to stop them, there were no locks on the bedroom doors.

4) In cross-examination, Park denied that by delaying reporting Carol missing in 1976 that he was "buying time". He was waiting for information from someone. He maintained that if he had wanted to murder his wife, he wouldn't have done it at the start of the school summer holidays when he had three children to look after!

5) After he had reported Carol as missing, he said that the police came into his home many times, looked in cupboards and drawers, and took away documents, but did not conduct the sort of systematic search that had been carried out at Norland Avenue.

6) He claimed that he had no boat "available" in July 1976. He had sold it in the June. He then agreed that the sailing log he kept referred to the sale as being in July. However, he said, the boat and the trailer would have been kept at Tower Wood near Windermere. He agreed that he had sailed it "on and off" on Coniston Water. He still maintained that he "did not know Coniston very well".

7) Regarding Mrs Young's evidence, he agreed that his boat was white but the description of the man in it could not apply to him as he did not wear glasses outside the home at that time. Shown a photograph of himself wearing glasses alfresco in 1973, however, he agreed he must have been wrong about that.

8) He had been shown photographs of the pinafore dress in which the body was recovered and agreed that it

A Very Cumbrian Murder

was similar to one that Carol used to wear. She did have a nightdress similar to a "baby-doll" one and she did sometimes sleep in a nightdress. He didn't, however, recognise the one in photographs he had been shown.

9) He agreed that he did own a chest freezer in July 1976, and, in cross-examination, also agreed that if he had been so inclined he could have stored a body in it.

10) He believed that in 1976 he and Carol had a joint account and that she also had her own account. He did not however put a stop on either, but would see the bank statements each month and watched them to see if there was any movement of money. As none was withdrawn or moved he assumed that someone else was supporting her.

11) He had no recollection of ever seeing Wainwright before seeing him in court during the trial.

12) Cross-examined about the time when he first learnt that Carol's body had been recovered, Park said that he didn't "feel the need" to phone the police or Carol's brother. He didn't communicate very much with the latter. He maintained that he couldn't have got home much quicker – the ferry was already booked and there were two Bed-and-Breakfasts booked. He denied that he needed "time".

In an atmosphere in court of almost unbearable tension, the jury returned from their deliberations on 28 January 2005. Their verdict of "Guilty" was unanimous.

In delivering sentence, Mr Justice McCombe, indicated that he was taking into account "the terrible concealment of the body". Gordon Park was sentenced to life imprisonment with a recommendation that he serve at least 15 years before he could be considered for parole.

***

The sentence was not the end of the matter as far as Park's family and supporters, and the judicial process, were concerned. New solicitors and counsel were instructed, and in December 2007, appeal against conviction was lodged. The appeal was based upon "fresh evidence that was not available at the trial", evidence that was "very strong and significant".

Three Court of Appeal judges, however, in November 2008, dismissed the appeal. Park's counsel wanted to call an expert witness to challenge the geological evidence used at the trial. In delivering the court's judgment, Lord Justice Keene said that the new evidence did not raise "a reasonable doubt as to the safety of the conviction". The geological evidence, he said, was only a small element of "the strong circumstantial case against the applicant".

After the failure of the appeal, Gordon's family and a band of supporters continued with a campaign to secure his release from prison. Jeremy set up a website – www.freegordon.com. Some notable individuals offered their support, including Tony Benn MP who described the verdict as a "grave injustice" and claimed there was considerable doubt about the conviction. Whether his view was based upon a familiarity with the evidence or simply hearsay, I do not know.

Over 300 people signed a petition headed 'Gordon Park is innocent'. Many millions, however, did not!

About 40 friends and family held a vigil at Strangeways prison in 2006, and further such vigils were held in 2007 and 2008, before the outcome of the appeal.

An evangelical pastor, George Harrison, with whom Gordon and Jenny Park had stayed during the trial, headed a campaign that offered a reward of £5000 for anyone providing evidence that resulted in Gordon's freedom. Jeremy Park, however, disassociated himself from this campaign.

Not everyone linked to the Park family supported his attempts to clear his name. Vanessa, for example, had given evidence for the prosecution at the trial. Ivor Price, after the verdict, said that he had "no doubt" that justice had been done. Sadly, both Ivor and Maureen Price had died before the appeal was rejected in 2008.

In prison, Gordon continued to maintain his innocence to the end. "The end" for him came at Garth prison, Leyland, on 25 January 2010, his sixty-sixth birthday, when he hanged himself in his cell...

Chapter Ten

No Smoke...

The strongest and most unapologetic case in favour of Gordon Park was advanced by Sandra Lean in her book published in 2007, *No Smoke! The Shocking Truth About British Justice*. As the title suggests, the author sets out to demolish the criminal justice system as a fair and effective process for establishing guilt, and seeks to demonstrate this by highlighting what she perceives as serious flaws in the investigations and trials in seven high profile cases in which persons were convicted of murder.

Dr Sandra Lean is an academic, with an honours degree in Psychology and Sociology and a PhD in Criminal Justice. She also has a specialist paralegal qualification in criminal law and is a fully qualified clinical hypnotherapist and hypno-analyst. For more than ten years she has researched and written about cases of wrongful conviction and factual innocence. The title of her PhD thesis was 'Hidden in Plain View', which studied the factors which led to wrongful convictions.

Impressive qualifications one may think, but these, of course, are all paper qualifications. The author is not and never has been a practising lawyer and does not, as far as I am aware, have any experience of any active involvement in criminal investigations or jury trials. To my, this undermines her credentials as any sort of expert on the subject of wrongful convictions or miscarriages of justice, and, indeed, her book, I believe, betrays a lack of appreciation of the realities of police investigations in murder cases and of the workings of the trial process and the jury system. Nonetheless, Dr Lean does not hold back from being severely critical of the police investigators, the prosecuting authorities or the trial processes in all these cases, including that of Regina versus Gordon Park.

It was my irritation and exasperation with her approach and forthright and self-satisfied conclusions that really led me to write this book, and to try to redress the balance against what I saw as an unwarranted and misconceived attack upon the integrity of the investigation in Park's case and, indeed, of his ultimate conviction.

By diligent and painstaking examination of evidence and trial transcripts, Dr Lean in her book has identified seven notorious murder cases from recent times where she claims that the defendants have been wrongly convicted. Her conclusions are based on this purely paper exercise – she has not witnessed the actual trials and heard the evidence being given in court and being tested in cross-examination. The seven cases she has selected, moreover, are hardly the best illustrations of "wrongful convictions": only in one of those cases has the conviction since been overturned, and in another the "wrongly convicted" defendant later admitted his guilt whilst serving his prison sentence!

In general terms, Dr Lean maintains that the criminal justice system in cases of homicide is seriously and fundamentally flawed for a number of different reasons, and at every stage of the process leading to a conviction:

1) Police investigations are flawed, she says, because they are routinely driven not by a <u>search for the truth</u> but by a <u>requirement to find someone to prosecute</u>. The result

of that approach is that a line of enquiry which may "lead to the truth, but is unlikely to lead to a prosecution, may be discarded in favour of that which may not be 'the truth' in the bigger picture, but fits more neatly with that which is likely to secure a prosecution". This approach is engendered by many factors – financial considerations, media attention, public pressure etc.

It is undoubtedly the case that the police are, in a homicide enquiry, subject to these and other internal and external pressures. To suggest, however, that investigations are pursued with complete tunnel vision and that obvious lines of enquiry are ignored is misconceived and insulting to the professionalism of police officers who are charged with the investigation of such serious matters. Such investigations must necessarily be focused, and experienced detectives, as a result of that unique experience and their training, will often have an instinct as to the likely culprit which will often be supported by the early evidence, and it is surely only right that they concentrate their efforts in that direction rather than engaging in a sprawling open-ended enquiry which is likely only to lead to blind alleys and cul-de-sacs. Sometimes, however, the investigation will throw up other potential suspects, and, as the Gordon Park case itself demonstrates, those suspects will be embraced by the enquiry.

At the end of the day, if the police find "someone to prosecute", the evidence must strongly support the guilt of that person, otherwise the prosecution is likely to fail. A criminal trial is weighted, from the outset, in favour of an accused. The jury will be instructed by both counsel, probably more than once, and by the judge, that they can only convict the defendant if they are <u>sure</u> of his or her guilt. There is a very heavy burden on the prosecution. There is no room for slippage or half-measures. The case must be proved <u>beyond reasonable doubt</u> and if the prosecution have got the wrong man it will almost certainly show...

2) Dr Lean claims that systems used by the police and prosecuting authority to disclose to the defence evidence and material which is not being used as part of the prosecution case are also flawed as they can lead to crucial evidence being denied to the defence team. Her observations, however, betray a lack of knowledge of how those systems operate.

Once the evidence is collected, she says, the police officer who is designated as the "disclosure officer" then "lists what evidence is deemed to be relevant, both for the prosecution and for the defence". If he or she deems it "irrelevant", then that evidence is "simply recorded in a separate list or schedule". But, she says, what he or she considers to be "relevant" might not be the same as what the defence consider to be "relevant".

This description of the role of the disclosure officer and the disclosure system is, however, quite misleading. The use of the word 'relevant' is unhelpful here as 'relevance' was a term that applied to the disclosure regime which existed before the coming into effect of the Criminal Procedure and Investigations Act 1996, but not thereafter. What we are talking about here is that evidence and material which has been gathered by the police in their investigation but which is not to form part of the body of evidence which goes to make up the prosecution case against the defendant. The latter is nothing to do with the disclosure officer and will be served upon the defence in any event. The disclosure officer will then consider the remaining evidence and material, the "unused" material, and will decide if it is capable of "undermining" the prosecution case or if it might assist the defence in the conduct of their case as he sees it. Relevance doesn't come into it! He or she will indeed list the material which "undermines" or "assists", and separately list the remaining material on another schedule. Both lists are forwarded to the Crown Prosecution Service, and, if the Crown Prosecutor assigned to the case agrees with what the disclosure officer has done, he or she will give the defence the "undermining" and "assisting" material and also a copy of the schedule containing the remaining material.

So far so good, one might think. But, Dr Lean goes on, this isn't satisfactory at all, because there might be material on the separate schedule which is helpful to the defence and the disclosure officer simply hasn't appreciated that or may have ignored the fact that it may assist the defence. Furthermore, how can the defence determine whether any material on the list helps the defendant when it is often inadequately described in the schedule? Moreover, although the defence team can ask to see any material on the schedule, in order to do so they must disclose the defendant's defence to the charge and give the reasons why they say they are entitled to see the material in question. By disclosing their defence, moreover, this plays into the hands of the prosecution who can then look for extra evidence to counter the defence.

Again, these assertions are, partially at least, misleading. In the first place, the disclosure officer may not know exactly what the defence is going to be, but the Crown Prosecutor who looks at the schedule, and who

A Very Cumbrian Murder

has also seen the prosecution evidence, will almost certainly be able to work out how the defendant is going to defend the charge against him or her, and will be able to consider the content of the schedule in this light. It is fair to say that in the past, and probably even now, items listed on the schedule may not convey sufficient information to identify whether or not they may be of assistance to the defence, but, in my experience, the more senior Crown Prosecutors who deal with murder cases will, from instinct and experience, be able to determine which particular items need to be physically examined, in order to decide whether they should be 'disclosed'. Personally, I have always found that there are usually a number of items which warrant specific examination, even if many of them are unlikely to be of assistance to the defence, and even then, if in doubt, one errs on the side of "disclosure".

As far as "revealing one's hand" and disclosing the defendant's defence is concerned, this is a matter of no consequence whatsoever. Firstly, as indicated above, the defence to the charge is likely to be obvious anyway in the majority of cases, from a perusal of the prosecution case. Secondly, in a Crown Court case, the defendant is obliged to identify his defence anyway, in the form of a Defence Statement which is handed to the prosecution and the court – if he/she does not then he/she runs the risk of having "adverse inferences" drawn against him/her by the jury; and it also enables the prosecution to conduct a further trawl of the "unused" material to ensure there is nothing there to assist that defence. It must be extremely rare for the prosecution to be so taken by surprise by a revealed defence that they need to go out and look for extra evidence to counter it. The defence will almost certainly have been anticipated by the time of charging the defendant and any additional evidence already sought if necessary. Essentially, therefore, there is nothing, or should be nothing, in the disclosure procedure that prejudices the defendant or puts him at a disadvantage – indeed, it is designed to be beneficial to him/her.

It is also worth pointing out that there are in practice further safeguards built in to the prosecution process, and indeed into the defence arrangements, which make failures in disclosure of helpful unused material even less likely. In a murder case, the Crown will almost certainly have as leading counsel an experienced Queen's Counsel, who will look at the unused material schedule and, if necessary, advise as to whether any further material on it should be disclosed to the defence. This is in addition to the examination that will have been carried out earlier by the responsible Crown Prosecutor and possibly also by junior counsel. Furthermore, in some cases, if there is a lot of unused material, a special 'disclosure counsel' will also have been instructed, whose role is exclusively to deal with disclosure issues. The defence, moreover, will also be in the hands of a Queen's Counsel who will also be casting a critical eye on the disclosure schedule, and if he or she believes there is more to be disclosed, he or she will bring this up with the Crown QC and further disclosure will probably happen.

Dr Lean asks that "since the objective of the… allocated QC is to secure a conviction, is it possible that…" prosecuting counsel "may inadvertently influence the disclosure officer's decisions as to what is deemed 'relevant' or not?" We have already dismissed the concept of 'relevance', but her understanding of the role of prosecuting counsel and the scope in practice of the part played by the disclosure officer in the trial process is completely wide of the mark. In reality the disclosure officer will have no influence over, or decision-making in connection with, disclosure issues once the conduct of the case is in the hands of prosecuting counsel. Decisions about disclosure will be made without reference to him. His job in effect will have long been done. Prosecuting counsel will not "influence" the disclosure officer at all – he will make his own decisions, in conjunction perhaps with his junior and the Crown Prosecutor, but with no-one else. And it is certainly not the case that his objective is solely to "secure a conviction". Anyone who has been involved in the trial process in the Crown Court knows that this is not the case!

It is right, and it is well-known, that in the 1970s and 1980s there were some notorious "wrongful convictions" in murder cases, convictions that were overturned because the prosecution had failed to disclose material to the defence which would have assisted the defendant or defendants to assert his or her innocence. Since then, however, systems have been developed to ensure that these mistakes are not repeated, and, although no system is infallible, it is far, far less likely now that the Crown does not comply with its responsibilities as far as disclosure is concerned.

3) Working her way through the component parts of the criminal investigative, prosecution and judicial process, Dr Lean has, as one might have by now come to expect, a jaundiced but misconceived view of the Crown Prosecution Service (CPS). This body takes over the conduct of the criminal case once the defendant has been charged by the police and has a statutory duty to examine the evidence and determine whether that evidence is sufficient to provide a "realistic prospect of conviction" for

any offence. If the evidence is not considered sufficient, the CPS must stop the prosecution. In fact, in a homicide case, the CPS will have seen the evidence before charge and, nowadays, will actually make the decision to charge or not, on the same criterion as above.

According to Dr Lean the role of the CPS does not, however, afford any real safeguard against cases with insufficient evidence getting into court. The CPS, she says, is "made up of human beings…" (no argument there!), but human beings "who are making decisions not only on the evidence presented to them, but through the filter of their own beliefs and persuasions". The CPS operates "from a slightly biased viewpoint – the underlying assumption is that the police are not going to present a case unless they feel it is strong enough to proceed to court…". So what the CPS do is "something of a box-ticking exercise…".

This clearly suggests that the CPS is simply a 'rubber-stamp' for the police position that there is sufficient evidence to proceed to charge and trial and that is incapable of making an independent decision about the sufficiency of evidence. If it's good enough for the police, it's good enough for the CPS!

Clearly no-one has told the police that this is the situation! Or indeed the CPS. There has always been a not insubstantial percentage of cases where the CPS do not agree that the case should proceed to charge, or to trial. At one time many police officers quite openly expressed the view that the acronym 'CPS' should be rebranded as the 'Criminals' Protection Society'. Far from being a 'rubber-stamp' the organisation was seen as an obstacle to what they perceived as the effective prosecution of offenders.

The reality is that the CPS is quite as able to exercise independent decision-making in murder cases as in any other sort of criminal case. From my own standpoint, in more than one such case I have had to tell the senior investigating officer that there is not enough evidence to charge.

4) As with the CPS, so with the jury. Dr Lean asserts that "since the jurors know that they would not be sitting on the case at all if the Crown Prosecution Service had not decided that there was enough evidence to proceed, the jury sets out from a slightly biased position – the belief that there is, theoretically, enough evidence to convict the person in the dock". How does this square, she asks, with the "presumption of innocence"? The jury starts out from the position that an authority with a great of deal of experience in these matters has examined all the evidence and decided that it is sufficient to convict.

This is a remarkable proposition and, if it were remotely true, there would be little point in defendants pleading "Not Guilty" and entrusting their fate to a jury because the dice are so loaded against them that their chances of acquittal would be slim indeed. There may be some jurors who, before the start of the trial, actually have the belief that if the police and the CPS bring the case then the accused must be guilty, but to suggest that jurors as a whole start with this sort of pre-conceived notion is to insult the intelligence of many of the people who sit on juries.

Even if it were true that jurors start with this bias or prejudice, then it is almost certain to be fairly quickly dispelled as the trial gets underway. The reality is that jury trials are weighted in favour of the defendant, not against him. From the outset the jury is going to be hit by prosecution counsel with these sort of soundbites: "The prosecution bring the case and it is the prosecution that has to prove it"; "You can only convict the defendant if you are sure of his guilt". Defence counsel will be delivering the same message in spades at the end of the case, and the last words the jury will hear will be from the judge, who will be giving them the same warnings. There is a heavy burden on the prosecution and the jury will be left in no doubt about that.

Statistics show that in 2011, of defendants who pleaded "Not Guilty" in the Crown Court, some 62% were subsequently acquitted. Of these, 69% didn't even require the jury to make a decision because acquittals were ordered or directed by the judge. Of those cases that actually needed a verdict by the jury, about 40% resulted in acquittal. Hardly a picture of a seriously flawed judicial system in which juries slavishly rubber-stamp the prosecution line!

There are other 'flaws' identified by Dr Lean in the criminal justice process but this is enough to be going on with. It should be fairly clear by now that Dr Lean sees little that is right in the way that the police, the prosecution authorities or the courts conduct themselves, and has little faith that the process will lead to the conviction of the right persons. She sees "wrongful convictions" everywhere and one of those is that of Gordon Park. It is to that case that we must now return, to witness how she applies the principles set out above to the investigation and prosecution that led to his conviction.

★ ★ ★

A Very Cumbrian Murder

Dr Lean sets out to do a complete demolition job on the Crown's case against Gordon Park, disparaging the police investigation, the evidence, the witnesses and even the media coverage. By the end of this chapter of her book, the uninformed reader must wonder how Park ever came to be charged, let alone how the jury could possibly come to the decision that he was guilty, or, indeed, how the Court of Appeal could have failed to overturn the conviction.

Her opening gambit is a stark statement that sets out her stall: "…this case is based purely on circumstantial evidence, and there is no evidence to link Gordon Park with the murder of his first wife".

What Dr Lean is saying here in fact echoes the views taken by my superiors at CPS which led to the case being discontinued in 1998. There was indeed no evidence that <u>directly</u> linked Park to the murder – no DNA, no scientific evidence, no identification of the killer, no confession, no 'smoking gun'. The case was based "purely on circumstantial evidence", but then we had never argued that it was otherwise, and this was the way it was presented to the jury in the trial.

The suggestion is that there is some stigma to cases founded on circumstantial evidence only, that such evidence is just not good enough, that it carries no weight. Nothing could be further from the truth. I have been involved in more than one murder case where there was only circumstantial evidence but convictions have resulted, convictions that have not been disturbed in subsequent appeals. I mentioned one such case in chapter eight – the case of Shatanawi, where there wasn't even a body! Another more recent case in which I was involved and, indeed, where I made the decision to charge the defendant was that of Robert Wilson.

Wilson's case has some parallels with that of Gordon Park. He too murdered his wife, tried to cover it up and would probably have got away with it had it not been for a stroke of good fortune, or misfortune in his case. Wilson had made a 999 call to the police to say that there had been a terrible accident, that he had run over his wife with his tractor whilst reversing the vehicle in the cowshed. The pathologist who did the post mortem endorsed this scenario as the likely cause of death and the police accepted that no further investigation was necessary. That, on the face of it, would have been the end of the matter, had not the adult children of the deceased not come across some greetings cards whilst they were retrieving some of their mother's possessions from her bedroom, whilst Wilson was absent from the house. The greeting cards were addressed to Wilson, they were from a lady called 'Kathy' and were clearly of an amatory nature. The children's suspicions were aroused and the cards were seized and in due course handed over to the police.

A police investigation did then ensue, and it was discovered that Wilson had been conducting an affair with a woman called Kathy that he had met in a bar in Spain. Not long before his wife's death he had also taken out a substantial insurance policy on her life. Kathy was tracked down and interviewed and it transpired that she was due to join Wilson at his farm in Kirkandrews-on-Eden, Cumbria, the very weekend that Mrs Wilson met her tragic end, but Wilson told her to delay her visit. He had told her that his wife had died from cancer some time previously.

A Very Cumbrian Murder

By this time there was no prospect of a further post mortem being conducted because Mrs Wilson's body had been cremated, but an eminent Home Office forensic pathologist examined photographs of the body and the scene of her supposed death and was of the opinion that Mrs Wilson was already dead when she was crushed by the wheels of the tractor, because of the absence of blood on or around the body. This evidence was not conclusive, however, and the case was presented as one based on the circumstantial evidence, that Wilson's "two worlds were about to collide" and he had no alternative but to dispose of his wife in order to enable his relationship with Kathy to continue in England. At one point the trial judge, Mr Justice Clarke, was moved to mention that he had "never known a case" based "so much on circumstantial evidence". The point was, however, that this evidence was compelling and the jury were able to return a unanimous verdict of "Guilty" to the charge of murder. Wilson was sentenced to life imprisonment with a recommendation that he serve at least 22 years before he was eligible for parole. His later appeal against conviction failed.

That the case against Gordon Park was based purely on circumstantial evidence is Dr Lean's central argument in her thesis that he was wrongfully convicted, and, as such, it is a weak and misconceived argument. It is worth restating that, in dismissing Park's appeal, the judges of the Court of Appeal stressed that there was a "strong circumstantial case" against the accused, and, clearly were not troubled, any more than were the jury, that there was no direct evidence linking him to the crime. Circumstantial evidence was not enough for Dr Lean; it was patently enough for the police, the prosecuting authority (latterly at least), prosecuting counsel, the trial judge, the jury and the Court of Appeal.

* * *

Dr Lean goes on to relentlessly attack specific parts of the evidence that the prosecution led against Park, but, although she makes some valid points, she tarnishes her case to some extent with a number of factual errors. She asserts as a fact, for example, that Carol did not go on the day trip to Blackpool because she "was feeling unwell". Gordon Park said this was not the reason, and there was no other first-hand evidence that it was.

She states that the Crown claimed that Gordon had not gone to Blackpool that day and that the story was a "cover"; and further that the prosecution claimed that he had drugged his wife and stored her body in a chest freezer before dumping it in Coniston Water. This she says was "complete speculation". She is right of course but it never happened. These events may have happened, or not happened as the case may be, but they were not supported by evidence and the prosecution could not and did not advance them as part of the case. There was evidence of a chest freezer in Park's garage, and Glen Banks claimed that Park told him that he had administered drugs to her whilst they were in the boat together, but Dr Lean seems to have welded these two disparate and irreconcilable strands together into an allegation that was never in fact made.

She also asserts that Carol had several affairs during her marriage, "including with a police officer and a solicitor". Whilst the first part of that statement is certainly true, she is not entitled to put forward the part in quotation marks as a fact, since the only reference to it comes from Park himself and even he cannot name his source, and accepts that it is hearsay and "tittle-tattle".

A Very Cumbrian Murder

She tries to undermine the evidence of the pathologist Dr Tapp by claiming that he is wrong when he says that the body must have been trussed up before rigor mortis set in, because, she says, this fails to take account of the fact that rigor passes within 24 to 48 hours so that the body could have been tied up at that point. She fails to acknowledge, however, that Dr Tapp covers this possibility by pointing out that there would have been a good deal of putrefaction by this time which would have been inconsistent with the degree of fatty tissue on the body.

★ ★ ★

Dr Lean ridicules the evidence of Mrs Young, who testified that, from a car park on the east side of Coniston Water, a few days after 25 July 1976, she had witnessed a man bearing the description of Park, tipping a package into the water from a boat. Whilst it is right that the evidence has limited value, to describe it as "vague, almost useless testimony" is clearly wrong. If the evidence matched that description, so that any evidential value it might have was eclipsed by its prejudicial effect, the trial judge would not have allowed it to have been given. The fact that the evidence was allowed to go before the jury is indicative of the fact that it did have some probative value. The jury might well have concluded from that evidence that they were hearing about the disposal of the body, bearing in mind that it closely corresponded with the manner in which the body was almost certainly abandoned in the lake.

Furthermore, says Dr Lean, if the Young evidence is accurate, and if it is Park that she saw, then he must have held on to the body for almost two weeks, and then also disposed of his boat almost immediately afterwards. This she asserts "does not make sense". Why not?! It seems to me that, on the contrary, it makes a lot of sense to get rid of the means of disposing of the body as soon as possible after the deed is done!

The evidence relating to stone and slate, allegedly recovered from the bed of the lake close to where the body lay, was "completely discredited" says Dr Lean. As discussed in chapter nine, this evidence was of limited and even dubious value, and one cannot argue with her general observations about it, even if she resorts to her by now consistent tendency to 'go over the top' with her language!

As one might expect, Dr Lean thinks very little of the evidence of Roger Ide and the nature of the knots used to truss up the body. This, for her, comes under the "completely discredited" umbrella. Comparisons with knots known to have been tied by Park, she says, "proved nothing of any worth" and the type of knots on the body "indicated a level of 'ability' which would have been common to a number of people, and not 'specialist knowledge'... as the prosecution had claimed". Again, however, she misses the point. The significance of this evidence is not to be gauged by taking it in isolation, but that Gordon Park, the man with the motive, the opportunity and the resources, had the "ability" to tie all the knots in question. It is another strand of the circumstantial case against him.

Dr Lean also points out that the jury were never told that Mike Lucas had retracted his original opinions about who had tied the knots. Of course they were not told, because the prosecution did not rely on his evidence. It was not, however, a case of the prosecution concealing his opinions – the defence were in possession of his statements and knew exactly what he had said and they knew how he had changed those views.

Nor is it any great surprise that Dr Lean is very dismissive of the "confession evidence" provided by Wainwright and Banks. She makes all the obvious points about the potential unreliability of their testimony, but on the other hand, as ever, her appraisal of the evidence amounts to a total whitewash. She sees no positive points about it whatsoever.

★ ★ ★

Given Dr Lean's general criticism of the way that the police conduct their investigations, it is inevitable that she finds fundamental flaws with the investigation in Park's case.

The police, in their investigation from 1997, did not "focus sufficiently on other men who may have had reason to become violent or jealous towards Carol Park". There were, she maintains, several men who could have fitted the description of the killer as set out by Alistair Webster in his opening address to the jury – ie. someone who knew her well enough to come across her in a short nightdress; a person who had cause to strongly dislike her or lose his temper with her; a person who was thoroughly familiar with knots, both as a sailor and a climber; a meticulous person; a person with access to a boat and familiarity with Coniston Water.

In the first place, she says, any of the men with whom Carol had had affairs would presumably have come across her in a nightdress. Moreover, one of them at least may have had cause to strongly dislike her because she had left him "on two occasions without warning" – ie. Brearley.

Apart from the fact that the evidence does not support the proposition that Brearley was left on either occasion without warning, the notion that he harboured feelings of rage or jealousy for 12 months and then murdered Carol is quite absurd. Nor is there any evidence that he was remotely interested in sailing or climbing, had any expertise in knot tying, had access to a boat or had any familiarity whatsoever with Coniston Water. Basically, he lacked the motive, opportunity, resources or expertise to carry out the deed, so why would he merit any further investigation than the limited one that was directed towards him?

Furthermore, according to Dr Lean, the knots in question would be known to other sailors or climbers and those who worked in the local shipyard. It seems unlikely to me that shipyard workers would routinely know how to tie figure-of-eight knots and do lashings, but it would be fair to say that there would be a large number of climbers and sailors in this part of south Cumbria. So why did the police not extend their investigation into Carol's death to include questioning every identifiable climber and sailor in the region? Did they try to track down every man with whom Carol might have had an affair in the nine or ten years before her disappearance in 1976? Did they seek out every boat-owner in the southern Lake District, particularly those who sailed on Coniston Water, and question them to as to their movements on 17 July 1976?

The answer to these questions is that to run such an open-ended, wide-ranging enquiry would have been futile and pointless, and so ridiculously time-consuming that it would never have reached a conclusion. A police investigation must surely have some focus if it is to be effective. There must be at least a modicum of evidence to justify investigating specific individuals. The police had some sort of profile of the person they were looking for, the profile set out by prosecuting counsel above, and whilst a good deal of people might have one or other of those characteristics, very few would have all of them.

Dr Lean says that the defendant was always the "prime suspect" in the eyes of the police and therefore they simply proceeded on the basis of gathering evidence to confirm their suspicions, and ignored other potential suspects. The point was of course that no other known potential suspects remotely matched the profile of the offender. Nor can one, I think, ignore the instincts of experienced detectives – those instincts told them that Park, and no-one else, was their man, so it is scarcely surprising that he was the person against whom the investigation was principally directed.

Ultimately, of course, it was a decision for the jury. The defence at the trial would strain every sinew to underline that there was no direct evidence against him, that others could not be ruled out of the equation, and that the jury had to be "sure" of Park's guilt before they could convict him. But convict him they did.

Gordon Park ticked every box, possessed every characteristic of the profile. He was not just the "prime suspect", he was the only suspect.

Dr Lean claims that the police did not adequately pursue the 'Blue Beetle' element of the enquiry, and more could have been done to identify the owner of the vehicle and its driver. The police, however, went to some lengths to do just this. At the end of the day the jury were in possession of this evidence and, if it was thought to have any significant bearing on the case, then no doubt it might have impacted on their verdict.

Inevitably, Dr Lean raises the spectre of John Rapson, his criminal history, and the possibility that he was at large in the area at the time of Carol's disappearance. She somehow comes to the conclusion that, as he apparently spent his early working life in the shipyard as a fitter or apprentice fitter, then he must have had knowledge of a wide range of knots and also "know his way around boats". Now who is speculating?! There wasn't a grain of evidence that he had any such knowledge, had any motive to kill Carol, or had the means or the resources to get to Leece at that time and carry out a murder and elaborate cover-up. Again, of course, the jury were aware of his history and whereabouts at the material time, but clearly did not attach any importance to these facts.

★ ★ ★

The media come in for a scathing attack by Dr Lean. She turns first to the press coverage of the case in 1997 and 1998, which, she says, was "intense, sensationalist and extremely prejudiced". Taking no prisoners there then! She maintains that the press coverage at this time contained "negative connotations, and thinly veiled hints... that Gordon 'had got away with it' purely because of the passage of time...". She claims that Gordon was portrayed in the press as "cold, calculating, controlling, and violent...". An enormous and uncompromising indictment of the press at this time, but not one that I recognise.

She goes on by saying that after the case was dropped in 1998, the press continued to print "ever more inaccurate and sensationalist articles". It was because of this, she says, that Gordon agreed to co-operate with the Daily Mail and give an "official" interview, in the hope that it would put an end to the "speculation and harassment". Despite what she says about the press, Dr Lean produces no evidence to support her accusations, and it is noticeable that Park himself is considerably more restrained – when interviewed by the police in 2004, he states that the press coverage had been "sensationalised" but only "somewhat inaccurate". There was certainly widespread press interest in the case in 1998, but the coverage certainly did not merit anything like the description of it given by Dr Lean.

Still on the subject of Gordon's "official" interview with the press, for which of course he was paid £50,000, Dr Lean claims that before the trial a "protocol" was agreed between the prosecution and the defence not to raise this matter before the jury. The Crown, however, she says, reneged on the deal and raised in court the issue of payment for the article in order to support an argument that Park was prepared to "profit" from the death of his wife, whilst, at the same time, neglecting to mention that Banks and Wainwright "did stand to profit from giving evidence against Gordon".

This, says Dr Lean, was only one example of the "dirty tricks" played by the prosecution in the trial, and one that "demands investigation".

Such an accusation I am tempted to regard as naïve rather than malicious. There was no "investigation" of course because no-one other than Dr Lean saw the need for one. If there ever was any such "protocol", then the notion that prosecuting counsel would openly breach it and that experienced leading counsel for the defence would stand idly by and allow it to happen without a word of objection, is totally absurd. Nor would a High Court judge permit the practice of a "dirty trick". If the issue of payment for the article was allowed in evidence then it was because it was considered 'relevant'. By the same token, neither Banks or Wainwright did in fact profit financially from giving evidence, so there was nothing to mention, and if it was considered that they had impure motives for testifying against Park, then the defence would have had the opportunity to raise this issue with them in cross-examination.

By implication at least, another "dirty trick" according to Dr Lean, was the decision of the prosecution to "ignore" the fact that being given custody of his children by the family court in the 1970s "casts serious doubts on the portrayal of Gordon as violent…". Again, this is a completely naïve statement. Even if such a conclusion could be drawn from the award of custody to Gordon, the defence were fully in possession of this information and it would be open to and up to defence counsel to present this argument to the jury. The suggestion that this was a "dirty trick" betrays a complete lack of awareness of the nature of the proceedings in a criminal trial.

Dr Lean also draws attention to the nature of the press coverage of Gordon's re-arrest in 2004. In particular, she highlights a piece in The Times on 14 January 2004, which states:

"Cumbria police said that the arrest had come after a further six years of state-of-the-art forensic science analysis and wider enquiries. Though the suspect has not been named officially, sources close to the investigation confirmed that it was Mr Park."

"In other words," says Dr Lean, "they always knew it was him, they just had to get enough evidence against him." This is surely prejudicial, bound to influence the jury, offends against the presumption of innocence, and what it says to the jury in fact is 'this man has been guilty for a very long time, and now we have evidence to prove it'.

The piece of course says nothing of the sort. Dr Lean is simply riding one of her favourite hobby-horses, her claim that the jury always start from a biased viewpoint because they are bound to infer that the defendant is guilty because the police and the CPS have gathered evidence that convinces them that this is the case. We looked at this earlier in this chapter and there is no merit in going over it again!

★ ★ ★

Coming to the end of her examination of the Park case, Dr Lean moves inexorably and assertively towards her inevitable conclusion – that the jury got it wrong, and that Gordon Park was wrongly convicted.

In summarising her position, she makes a number of correct and obvious points, but also resorts to the sort of speculation in which she previously had accused the prosecution of indulging.

Gordon could not have been convicted on the basis of "eyewitness testimony" she says, because there isn't any. There are no confirmed sightings which related him to the murder of his wife. Correct.

There was, she points out, no physical, forensic or DNA evidence linking him to the crime, so he could not have been convicted on the strength of such evidence. Again correct.

Nor, she says, was he convicted on the basis of previous behaviour proving him to be likely to resort to the type of behaviour involved in the accusations against him. Here, Dr Lean, is talking about violent behaviour towards Carol during their marriage, and it is fair to say that there is no evidence of such, and no evidence that he had any propensity towards brutally murdering his wife. On the subject of 'behaviour', however, there was evidence of a 'dark side', of a manipulative, controlling personality. Also of a man with an obsession with detail and meticulousness. Might not the jury have taken into account these aspects of his behaviour when considering their verdict?

Dr Lean claims that Gordon was not "convicted because of the absence or elimination of other possible suspects". But how can she possibly know this? Simply because she might regard someone like John Rapson as a "possible suspect" and simply because no-one could account for his whereabouts at the time of Carol's disappearance, this is not to say that the jury took any account of this. Indeed, had the jury seriously regarded the possibility of a third party as being the killer, then presumably they would not have been satisfied beyond reasonable doubt of Park's guilt?

On the issue of the knots, Dr Lean maintains that the knots used to truss the body were "not specialist" but were "…quite common". There was no link established between Gordon and the knots, so he "was not, then, convicted on the grounds of association with specialist knowledge". At the risk of stating the obvious, of course it is true that the jury could not have convicted Park on such grounds alone, but it would be highly speculative and presumptuous to suggest that the jury did not find the fact that he could tie all these knots as very significant when taken in conjunction with all the other evidence. The knots may have been "common" in sailing and climbing circles, but not to the majority of the population, so there is some "specialist knowledge" here. The jury would have been very aware of the very elaborate way that the body was trussed and the attention to detail involved, that access to a boat and an aptitude for sailing would have been required to jettison the body, that the person responsible clearly wanted to ensure that the body would never be found, that he or she in all probability was intimate enough with the deceased to encounter her in her nightdress... If Park, for the jury, ticked all these boxes, then they could surely hardly ignore the fact that he was a sailor and an ex-climber, and had the knowledge and expertise to tie all the knots involved.

Dr Lean is at her most speculative and presumptuous, however, when it comes to the evidence of the "cell confessions". Whilst she might legitimately summarise the evidence of Banks and Wainwright as "dubious testimony", how can she possibly conclude that Park "was not convicted on the grounds of the confessions he is claimed to have made"? Without being a fly on the wall in the jury room, how can she possibly know how the jury regarded this evidence? They may, of course, for all we know, have convicted on the basis of this evidence alone! The answer of course is that Dr Lean is never troubled with such possibilities. If she thinks the evidence is worthless, then the jury must have thought the same. She completely discounts the possibility that the jury may have taken a view of the evidence that does not accord with her own!

We now reach her ultimate conclusion, the apogee of her argument. Having discounted and dismissed all the evidence led by the prosecution, it is inevitable that she then poses the question "On what basis *was* Gordon Park convicted?" She doesn't need to answer the question, of course, because, as far as she is concerned, the conviction was wrong. "From the evidence presented, Gordon Park has not been proven guilty of anything, far less proven guilty 'beyond reasonable doubt.'"

But wait a minute, I hear you cry - isn't it a matter for the jury, and no-one else, whether the prisoner has been proved guilty "beyond reasonable doubt", and this jury has found him guilty "beyond reasonable doubt". So in the last analysis Dr Lean is quite wrong, because Park has been proved guilty to that exacting standard of proof by the one body entrusted with that decision. Dr Lean, however, knows better than the collective wisdom of those '12 good men and true'!

★ ★ ★

Whatever merits Sandra Lean's book and her appraisal of the evidence in the Park case may have, they are, to my mind, completely eclipsed by her entrenched and overwhelming antagonism towards and her disdain for the way that the organs of the criminal justice system operate and conduct their affairs. Her simple belief is that this system is quite incapable of preventing wrongful convictions. Her views might be more palatable if she even occasionally acknowledged some value, some force for good, in the system. Instead we get a complete whitewash. Nowhere is this more apparent than in the way she sets about the police investigation, the conduct of the prosecution, the evidence, and the verdict of the jury, in the Park case. The investigation is flawed and incomplete, the prosecution are guilty of "dirty tricks", the evidence is unreliable, dubious, inconclusive and ultimately totally inadequate, and the jury have just got it plain wrong. The book was published before Gordon Park's appeal was determined, but no doubt the Court of Appeal would have got it wrong as well! How she would have shuddered at the learned judges' assertion that there was a "strong circumstantial case".

Dr Lean seems completely consumed by a sense of her own infallibility. She sets herself up as someone who knows better than any other player in the criminal justice system – better than the police, the prosecution authority, prosecution counsel, the judges and the jury. This is pure hubris. It is unbecoming in and unacceptable from a person who, at the end of the day, is an academic, and someone who clearly has little insight into how police investigations have to work, what goes on in court, and, indeed, what evidence is sufficient to found a conviction in a murder trial. It is this unbalanced, partisan, uninformed, and arrogant stance on the part of the author that, to my mind, undermines the credibility of the book and prevents it from being treated as a serious work.

★ ★ ★

It is almost 40 years now since Carol Park was brutally murdered in the prime of her life. It is nearly 20 years since her remains were recovered from the murky depths of Coniston Water. It is more than ten years since Gordon Park was finally convicted of her murder, and six years since he put an end to his own life. Some of his close family may continue in their efforts to have his conviction overturned, but despite that, and despite the strident campaigns of Dr Sandra Lean and others, that conviction remains unshaken. Carol's brother, her only surviving sibling at the time of her death, has also gone, but at least he went to his grave with the satisfaction, if that is the right word, of knowing that his sister's killer had been brought to justice.

The jury clearly had no doubt about Park's guilt, and that is a certainty that I have always shared, or at least from the time of the 1997 investigation. Leaving aside so-called prison-cell confessions, lack of identification, forensic and scientific evidence, the bedrock of the case has always been for me, as the Court of Appeal put it, that "strong circumstantial case". The killer was no stranger, but someone who had an overwhelming need to try to ensure that Carol Park was never found, someone who was intimate enough with her to find her in a short nightdress, someone who had the inclination and the expertise to make an elaborate job of trussing up her body, someone who had the resources, expertise and local knowledge to dispose of her in Coniston Water, and someone who had the opportunity to murder her in the very short time-frame in which she was almost certainly killed. There is only one candidate on the shortlist, and there has never been another. The guilt of Gordon Park shines out like a beacon.

onmentally friendly book printed and bound in England by www.printondemand-worldwide.com

PEFC Certified

This product is
from sustainably
managed forests
and controlled
sources

www.pefc.org

PEFC/16-33-415

made of chain-of-custody materials; FSC materials for the cover and PEFC materials for the text pages.

f # - C0 - 197/132/18 - PB - Lamination Gloss - Printed on 18-Sep-18 21:51